Traditional foods in the Near East

FAO
FOOD
AND
NUTRITION
PAPER

50

Edited by
Shawky M. Dagher

FOOD
AND
AGRICULTURE
ORGANIZATION
OF THE
UNITED NATIONS
Rome, 1991

The designations employed and the presentation of material in this publication do not imply the expression of any opinion whatsoever on the part of the Food and Agriculture Organization of the United Nations concerning the legal status of any country, territory, city or area or of its authorities, or concerning the delimitation of its frontiers or boundaries.

M-76
ISBN 92-5-102982-2

All rights reserved. No part of this publication may be reproduced, stored in a retrieval system, or transmitted in any form or by any means, electronic, mechanical, photocopying or otherwise, without the prior permission of the copyright owner. Applications for such permission, with a statement of the purpose and extent of the reproduction, should be addressed to the Director, Publications Division, Food and Agriculture Organization of the United Nations, Via delle Terme di Caracalla, 00100 Rome, Italy.

© FAO 1991

Foreword

Traditional foods are an important component of people's diet and the basis for their food habits and nutrition. They also constitute an essential aspect of their cultural heritage and relate closely to people's historical background and to the environment in which they live. During the last few decades, the development of international food trade and the extensive urbanization process which have affected life-styles to a large extent in many parts of the world have resulted in a sizeable decrease in the consumption of traditional foods and a relative neglect in the cultivation of traditional food crops. The governing bodies of FAO have recommended that FAO give due consideration in its programme to the promotion of the production and consumption of traditional foods worldwide. Accordingly, several studies and projects have been initiated by FAO in different parts of the world to survey existing traditional foods and food crops, study their nutritional values and identify ways and means of promoting their production and consumption.

The Near East region has a wealth of traditional foods whose origins go as far back as the time of the Pharaohs in Egypt, the Phoenicians in the eastern Mediterranean and the Carthaginians in North Africa. The number and variety of civilizations that have passed through the region at one time or another in history have all left their mark on the eating habits and traditions of the various populations.

In recent years, as a result of increased food imports into the region, the consumption of traditional foods has diminished considerably and many of these foods are disappearing under the invasion of imported easy-to-prepare, processed and semi-processed foods.

It was decided therefore that a study should be carried out to document existing traditional foods in the region and to assess their nutritional value and contribution to the diet.

In cooperation with the FAO Regional Office for the Near East and with the assistance of selected consultants from the region, the Food Policy and Nutrition Division conducted four subregional studies on traditional foods in North Africa, Egypt and the Sudan, the eastern Mediterranean region, and the Gulf. These studies were reviewed in September 1989 by a panel of experts at a technical consultation which had the task of evaluating the content of the subregional studies and of combining them in one single document for the entire region. In doing so, the consultation had to consider the following criteria:

- only those traditional foods documented in the scientific literature were to be retained;
- simple, non-processed crops were to be eliminated;
- food preparation and recipes were also to be eliminated; and
- emphasis was to be given to those traditional foods that present potential for commercial/industrial production.

The present document is the final outcome of the work of the consultation.

While it is recognized that the information contained in this document is far from being exhaustive, as there are many traditional foods that are not cited in the literature, it is hoped that its publication will encourage nutritionists, food scientists, and food technologists in the region to give this subject more attention and to develop appropriate technologies for the industrial production and commercial distribution of these foods.

This work would not have been possible without the technical input of the authors of the above-mentioned four subregional studies:

Dr Mohammed Mansour for the study on North Africa

Dr Mohammed H. Ragab for the study on Egypt and the Sudan

Dr Shawky Dagher for the study on the eastern Mediterranean

Dr Abdul Rahman Musaiger for the study on the Gulf.

Comments on the content of the document and proposals for inclusion in subsequent revisions should be addressed to:

Dr E. Boutrif
Food Science Officer
Food Policy and Nutrition Division
Room C294, FAO
Via delle Terme di Caracalla
00153 Rome
Italy

Contents

Foreword	iii
1. CEREALS AND LEGUMES	**1**
Bread	**1**
Arabic bread	1
Fino bread	3
Samouli bread	4
Thin pan bread	5
Yemeni bread	7
Flat bread	7
Kesra	9
Kisra	10
Date bread	11
Other cereal-based foods	**13**
Kaak and *kaak b'zaatar*	13
Burghol	13
Melthuth and *tchicha*	15
Freekeh or *fereek*	16
Mirmiz or *frik*	17
Couscous	19
Mhammas	21
Saykouk	23
Hlalim	23
Ftaier	25
Uhbik	26

Rghaief	27
Shâariya	28
Foods based on cereal-legume mixtures	**29**
Bsissa	29
Assidat homs	31
Koshary and *mjaddarah*	32
Legume foods	**34**
Foul mdammas	34
Leblebi	36
Bisara	37
Falafel	39
Hommos b'tehineh	40
Lentils	41
Lupine seeds	43
Fenugreek seeds	44
2. MILK AND MILK PRODUCTS	**53**
Fresh milk	**53**
Camel milk	53
Fermented milks	**53**
Zabady	53
Laban or *rayeb*	55
Lben	56
Labneh	58
Gemead	59
Kishk	60
Uggot or *madeer*	61
Cheeses	**62**
Domiati cheese	62

Kariesh cheese	65
Mish	67
Halloum cheese	70
Nabulsi cheese	70
Shankleesh	71
Yemeni cheese	72
Butter	**73**
Ghee	73
3. MEAT, FISH AND THEIR PRODUCTS	**77**
Raw meat	**77**
Camel meat	77
Cured meat products	**77**
Pastirma or *bastorma*	77
Kadide	80
Shermute	81
Sausages	**82**
Naqaneq	82
Sujuk	83
Iraqi *bastirma*	84
Merguez	85
Other meat products	**86**
Lakhliâa	86
Qawarma	87
Fermented fish	**89**
Feseekh	89
Mehiawah	90
Tareeh	91

Dried fish	92
Samak or *mujaffaf*	92
Brined fish	94
Salted sardines	94
Melouha	95

4. FRUITS AND VEGETABLES — 99

Fruits	99
Dates and date products	99
Grape products	101
Carob	104
Pomegranate extract	106
Quamareddeen	107
Citrus products	109
Jujube	111
Doum	111
Vegetables	112
Baba ghannouj	112
Brined grape leaves	114
Dried okra	115
Crushed green olives	116
Harissa or *hrouss*	117
Felfel zina or *felfla*	118
Slata meshwiya	119
Dukkous	120

5. BEVERAGES, SWEETS AND CONFECTION — 125

Beverages	125
Licorice extract	125
Karkade	127

Qahwah	128
Tamr hindi	129
Hulu mur	130

Sweets and confection	**131**
Halwa	131
Nashab	132
Halawa tehineyah	133
Hommosiyah, semsamiyah and *fouliyah*	135
Sambosa helwah	138
Mesfuf, rfissa and *seffa*	139
Droo or *sohlob*	140
Makrudh	141
Baklawah	142
Halkoum	144
Manna	145

Other food products	**146**
Tehineh	146
Orange-blossom water	148
Thyme	148
Mattay	150
Pumpkin preserve	151

Annex tables	**155**

Tables

Table 1
Proximate gross composition of Arabic bread   2

Table 2
Proximate gross composition and mineral content of *fino* bread   4

Table 3
Proximate gross composition and mineral content of *samouli* bread   5

Table 4
Proximate gross composition and mineral content of thin pan bread   6

Table 5
Proximate gross composition and mineral content of Yemeni bread   8

Table 6
Proximate gross composition and mineral content of flat bread   9

Table 7
Proximate gross composition of *kesra*   10

Table 8
Proximate gross composition and mineral content of date bread   12

Table 9
Proximate gross composition of *kaak*   14

Table 10
Proximate gross composition of *burghol*   15

Table 11
Proximate gross composition of *melthuth* and *tchicha*   16

Table 12
Proximate gross composition of *freekeh*   18

Table 13
Proximate gross composition of *mirmiz* or *frik*   19

Table 14
Proximate gross composition of couscous   21

Table 15
Proximate gross composition of *mhammas*   22

Table 16
Proximate gross composition of *saykouk*   24

Table 17
Proximate gross composition of *hlalim*   25

Table 18
Proximate gross composition of *ftaier*   26

Table 19
Proximate gross composition of *uhbik*   27

Table 20
Proximate gross composition of *rghaief*   28

Table 21
Proximate gross composition of *shâariya*   29

Table 22
Proximate gross composition of *bsissa*   31

Table 23
Proximate gross composition of *assidat homs*   32

Table 24
Proximate gross composition and mineral content of *koshary*   33

Table 25
Proximate gross composition of *foul mdammas*   36

Table 26
Proximate gross composition of *leblebi*   37

Table 27
Proximate gross composition and mineral content of *bisara*   38

Table 28
Proximate gross composition of *falafel*   40

Table 29
Proximate gross composition of lentils   42

Table 30
Proximate gross composition of raw and debittered lupine seeds   44

Table 31
Proximate gross composition and nutritive value of dry and germinated fenugreek seeds — 45

Table 32
Proximate gross composition and mineral content of camel milk — 54

Table 33
Proximate gross composition and mineral and vitamin content of *zabady* — 55

Table 34
Proximate gross composition and mineral content of *laban* — 56

Table 35
Proximate gross composition of *lben* — 58

Table 36
Proximate gross composition of *labneh* — 59

Table 37
Proximate gross composition of *kishk* — 61

Table 38
Proximate gross composition and mineral content of *uggot* — 63

Table 39
Proximate gross composition of *domiati* cheese — 65

Table 40
Proximate gross composition and nutritive
value of *kariesh* cheese   67

Table 41
Proximate gross composition and nutritive
value of *mish*   69

Table 42
Proximate gross composition of *shankleesh*   72

Table 43
Proximate gross composition of *ghee*   74

Table 44
Proximate gross composition and mineral
content of camel meat   78

Table 45
Proximate gross composition of *pastirma*   79

Table 46
Proximate gross composition of *kadide*   81

Table 47
Proximate gross composition of *naqaneq*   82

Table 48
Proximate gross composition of fresh
and dried *merguez*   86

Table 49
Proximate gross composition of *lakhliâa*   87

Table 50
Proximate gross composition of *qawarma* — 88

Table 51
Proximate gross composition of *feseekh* — 90

Table 52
Proximate gross composition of *mehiawah* — 91

Table 53
Proximate gross composition and mineral content of *tareeh* — 92

Table 54
Proximate gross composition and mineral content of some fish consumed in the Arabian Gulf — 93

Table 55
Proximate gross composition and mineral content of salted sardines — 94

Table 56
Proximate gross composition and nutritive value of *melouha* — 95

Table 57
Proximate gross composition of carob molasses — 105

Table 58
Proximate gross composition and nutritive value of carob pods — 106

Table 59
Proximate gross composition of *quamareddeen*   108

Table 60
Proximate gross composition of fresh
and dried lemons   110

Table 61
Proximate gross composition and mineral
content of jujube   112

Table 62
Proximate gross composition and nutritive
value of *doum*   113

Table 63
Proximate gross composition of brined
grape leaves   115

Table 64
Proximate gross composition of dried okra   116

Table 65
Proximate gross composition of green olives   117

Table 66
Proximate gross composition of *harissa*   118

Table 67
Proximate gross composition of *felfel zina*   119

Table 68
Proximate gross composition of *slata meshwiya*   120

Table 69
Proximate gross composition and mineral
content of *dukkous* — 121

Table 70
Proximate gross composition and nutritive
value of licorice — 126

Table 71
Proximate gross composition and nutritive
value of *karkade* — 128

Table 72
Proximate gross composition and nutritive
value of *tamr hindi* — 130

Table 73
Proximate gross composition of *halwa* — 132

Table 74
Proximate gross composition of *nashab* — 133

Table 75
Proximate gross composition and nutritive
value of *halawa tehineyah* — 135

Table 76
Proximate gross composition and nutritive
value of hard seed-coated candy — 138

Table 77
Proximate gross composition of *sambosa helwah* — 139

Table 78
Proximate gross composition of some kinds
of sweet couscous   140

Table 79
Proximate gross composition of *droo*   141

Table 80
Proximate gross composition of *makrudh*   142

Table 81
Proximate gross composition of *baklawah*   143

Table 82
Proximate gross composition of *manna*   145

Table 83
Mean composition and nutritive
value of white and red *tehineh*   147

Table 84
Proximate gross composition of green thyme   149

Table 85
Proximate gross composition of *mattay*   150

Table 86
Proximate gross composition of pumpkin
preserve   151

Annex table A1
Different types of bread used to varying
extents in several countries of the Near East   157

Annex table A2
Some cereal or legume-based foods
in common use in various countries
of the Near East   159

Annex table A3
Some milk products produced in
various countries of the Near East   161

Chapter 1
Cereals and legumes

BREAD
Arabic bread

Arabic bread *(khoubez arabi)* is very popular in many countries of the Near East and is known in Egypt as *shamy* bread. The flat, circular, bilayered loaves range in diameter from 10 to 30 cm, and their layers range from 0.5 to 1.5 cm in thickness. The pocket form of this bread allows it to be easily wrapped into a sandwich or divided into small pieces and used as a vehicle to transport food into the mouth.

Preparation. Flour of medium strength is quite suitable for preparing this kind of bread. The process of bread preparation is now almost totally mechanized in commercial bakeries, and the quality of bread may very well be a direct reflection of the quality of flour used in its preparation.

The flour is usually sifted before adding water, salt and yeast at the levels of 50, 1.5 and 1 percent respectively. The ingredients are then mixed for a period of 15-20 minutes, until a smooth, continuous dough mass is obtained. Fermentation starts shortly after mixing is completed and continues until the yeast is killed by the heat of the oven. The dough rises because of the production of carbon dioxide gas, which is caught in the gluten network. The dough mass is allowed a bulk fermentation of about ten minutes, after which it is passed through a divider that cuts the dough into cylindrical pieces about the size of a tennis ball. The dough pieces are allowed another ten-minute fermentation period before they are moulded into flat, thin, circular sheets.

The dough sheets are allowed a final fermentation time of about 45 minutes at 40°C and high relative humidity. Shortly before baking, the dough sheets are turned over and introduced into an oven maintained at

TABLE 1
Proximate gross composition of Arabic bread
(value per 100 g edible portion)

Component	Value
Energy value *(kcal)*	279
Moisture *(g)*	30
Protein *(g)*	8
Lipids *(g)*	1
Ash *(g)*	2
Crude fibre *(g)*	0.5
Nitrogen-free extract *(g)*	58

450-500°C. When exposed to the high temperature, the flat pieces of dough puff up and separate into two layers. Baking requires 30-90 seconds, depending on the thickness of the dough sheets and the temperature of the oven. The cooled bread is then packaged into thin, low-density polyethylene bags.

A bread known in Jordan as thick *kmaj* is very similar to Arabic bread, except that the dough sheets are rolled to about 2 cm thickness before final proofing and baking. The resulting heavier pockets resist staling and dehydration in the dry climate prevailing in Jordan better than the thin Arabic bread would. Egyptian *baladi* bread is very similar to thick kmaj except that the bread is dusted during the final stages of rolling and proofing with fine wheat bran instead of wheat flour.

Nutritive value. Bread is the staple food for most of the peoples of the Near East. It is considered a good source of energy because of its high content of carbohydrates. The protein quality of wheat has been confirmed to be of rather poor quality, because it is low in lysine, an essential amino-acid. Table 1 depicts the nutritive value of Arabic bread.

Fino bread

Egyptian *fino* bread resembles French bread in appearance. It is also called *sammoun* bread in Iraq and the Republic of Yemen and *armani* bread in Jordan. The long, semi-cylindrical loaves are baked in different sizes and weights, and are characterized by a hard, brown crust with white inner pulp.

Preparation. Fino bread is usually made from low-extraction-rate wheat flour using either the indirect or the direct process. In the indirect process, which is usually adopted in winter, half of the required quantity of yeast is used for the preparation of the sponge, and the other half is left for the main dough. For the preparation of the sponge, a mixture of 25 kg flour, 0.5 kg yeast and 16 litres water are mixed for half an hour, and the resulting dough is left for eight hours at room temperature to form the sponge. The main dough is made by mixing the sponge with 100 kg flour, 35 litres water, 1-1.5 kg sugar and 0.5 kg yeast, and mixing is continued for half an hour. The resulting dough is left to proof at room temperature for a period of four hours. The loaves are then shaped as desired and left for another half hour to proof, after which they are baked at 250°C for 15-30 minutes.

In the direct process, the step of preparing the sponge is omitted, and the main dough is directly prepared using the whole quantity of yeast: 1 kg yeast with 100 kg flour, 60 litres water, 1.5 kg salt and 1 kg sugar. The mixing process is continued for half an hour, followed by proofing at room temperature for one hour and a half. The loaves are then shaped and proofed for an additional hour and finally baked at 250°C for 15 minutes.

Recently, automatic bakeries have been put into operation in many countries of the Near East and are gradually replacing the traditional ones. Traditional, commercially baked bread is marketed in Egypt unwrapped and is known for its low keeping quality and tendency for rapid staling. Standardization and full mechanization of the bread-making process would improve its quality and facilitate its marketing.

The chemical composition of fino bread made from wheat flour of 82 percent extraction is shown in Table 2.

TABLE 2
Proximate gross composition and mineral content of *fino* bread made from wheat flour of 82 percent extraction
(value per 100 g, dry-weight basis)

Component	Value
Energy value *(kcal)*	333
Moisture *(g)*	35
Protein *(N x 5.7) (g)*	10
Lipids *(ether extract) (g)*	0.5
Ash *(g)*	2.2
Crude fibre *(g)*	0.3
Reducing sugars *(g)*	1.8
Starch *(g)*	70
Calcium *(mg)*	27.5
Phosphorus *(mg)*	198.36
Iron *(mg)*	3.97
Phytic acid phosphorus *(mg)*	36.4

Samouli bread

Samouli bread (*khoubez samouli*) is commonly consumed in the Kingdom of Saudi Arabia. It is similar to fino bread in Egypt and is made in oblong shapes in varying sizes. It is usually eaten at breakfast or used for the preparation of sandwiches.

Preparation. Samouli bread is prepared from a 1:2 mixture of wheat flour of extraction rates of 75 percent and 85 percent respectively. The flour is mixed with water, active dry yeast and salt for 15 minutes. The dough is allowed a bulk fermentation for 30 minutes. The dough is then moulded and fermented in trays on which oil is spread. It is baked at 200-225°C for 20 minutes. The final product has a brown crust and a white crumb. The average weight of the small-size loaf is 107 g.

TABLE 3
Proximate gross composition and mineral content of *samouli* bread
(value per 100 g edible portion)

Component	Value
Energy value *(kcal)*	257
Moisture *(g)*	36.9
Protein *(g)*	9.2
Lipids *(g)*	2.2
Ash *(g)*	1.1
Crude fibre *(g)*	0.6
Carbohydrates *(g)*	50
Calcium *(mg)*	38
Phosphorus *(mg)*	108
Iron *(mg)*	2.5
Sodium *(mg)*	357
Zinc *(mg)*	0.9

Nutritive value. The process of spreading vegetable oil on the trays increases the level of fat in the product through the absorption of oil by the bread. Lysine and threonine were found to be the first and second limiting amino-acids in samouli bread. For its composition, see Table 3.

Thin pan bread
Khoubez al-riqaq is a traditional thin pan bread usually prepared at home by some families or by street vendors. People purchase this bread directly from homes or from the local market (which in turn depends on home preparation). Recently some modern bakeries have begun producing this bread but on a small scale, because its consumption remains limited to a few social occasions. Khoubez al-riqaq is especially eaten during the Muslim fasting month, *Ramadan*.

TABLE 4
Proximate gross composition and mineral content of thin pan bread
(value per 100 g edible portion)

Component	Value
Energy value *(kcal)*	372
Moisture *(g)*	6.5
Protein *(g)*	12.5
Lipids *(g)*	0.4
Ash *(g)*	0.8
Crude fibre *(g)*	–
Carbohydrates *(g)*	79.8
Calcium *(mg)*	17
Phosphorus *(mg)*	231
Iron *(mg)*	1.8
Sodium *(mg)*	359
Zinc *(mg)*	1.7

Preparation. A high-extraction-rate wheat flour is generally used in the preparation of khoubez al-riqaq. The flour is mixed with salt and water until a dough of loose consistency is formed. A handful of dough is then spread (in a very thin layer) by hand on the top of a heated iron pan (*tawah*). When the edges of the dough start drying and lifting from the pan surface, the bread is removed with a knife and folded in half or in quarters. Sometimes an egg, some sugar and cardamom are added to the piece of dough while it is on the pan. This sweet bread is commonly eaten with tea or at *sahoor* (the meal before sunrise in Ramadan).

Nutritive value. This bread can be of good nutritive value when supplemented with eggs. Table 4 illustrates its composition.

Yemeni bread

Yemeni bread (*khoubez tannouri*) is consumed in Saudi Arabia, particularly in the central area. It is a circular, single-layered bread and is made from wheat flour.

Preparation. This bread is prepared from flour, salt, yeast and water. A proportion of 1:2 of flours of extraction rates 75 percent and 85 percent respectively are used. For preparation, the flour is first mixed with water. Other ingredients are then added and mixed well for 15 minutes. The dough is allowed to undergo bulk fermentation for 45 to 60 minutes, and is then cut into small pieces, rounded, flattened and baked at 450-500°C for 15 seconds. The average weight of the final product is about 190 g per piece.

Nutritive value. Yemeni bread shows relatively lower niacin level when compared to other Saudi breads, probably due to the lower amount of yeast added. Lysine and threonine are the first and second limiting amino–acids in Yemeni bread. Its nutritive value is shown in Table 5.

Flat bread

Flat bread (*khoubez tanoor* or *khoubez irani*) was introduced into the Arabian Gulf countries by Iranians and is very similar to the Iranian bread known as *taftoon*. It has become one of the most common breads consumed at breakfast and dinner in Bahrain, Qatar, Kuwait and the United Arab Emirates.

Preparation. Wheat flour is used in the preparation of tanoor bread. The extraction rate of the flour varies from country to country. In Kuwait, for example, a high-extraction-rate flour (90 percent) is used, while in Bahrain the extraction rate is lower (80 percent).

Tanoor bread is prepared by dissolving yeast (1.2 g), salt (13 g) and sodium bicarbonate (3 g) in 550 g water. One kg of flour is then added and mixed for 15 minutes. The dough obtained is cut into pieces, rounded, flattened and baked at 400-500°C in earthen ovens for 30-60 seconds. The final product

TABLE 5
Proximate gross composition and mineral content of Yemeni bread
(value per 100 g edible portion)

Component	Value
Energy value *(kcal)*	270
Moisture *(g)*	31.6
Protein *(g)*	10.1
Lipids *(g)*	0.3
Ash *(g)*	0.8
Crude fibre *(g)*	0.4
Carbohydrates *(g)*	56.8
Calcium *(mg)*	24
Phosphorus *(mg)*	112
Iron *(mg)*	2.5
Sodium *(mg)*	112
Zinc *(mg)*	1.2

is a circular bread composed of one layer, with an average loaf weight of 100 g (in Bahrain), and of 150 g (in Kuwait).

The short fermentation period of tanoor bread affects the utilization of iron and possibly other minerals. Fermentation increases the destruction of phytic acid, which adversely affects the bioavailability of iron, zinc and calcium. The use of sodium bicarbonate also has been found to inhibit phytic-acid destruction during bread preparation. Elimination of Nabicarbonate from the preparation formula and increasing the fermentation time are highly recommended to improve the quality of the bread.

Lysine and threonine are the first and second limiting amino-acids in this bread. However, tanoor breads are never consumed alone; they are usually eaten with other foods, such as meat and fish, which supplement the nutritional value of the bread (see Table 6).

TABLE 6
Proximate gross composition and mineral content of flat bread
(value per 100 g edible portion)

Component	Value
Energy value *(kcal)*	278
Moisture *(g)*	29.5
Protein *(g)*	8.4
Lipids *(g)*	1.2
Ash *(g)*	1.9
Crude fibre *(g)*	0.5
Carbohydrates *(g)*	58.5
Calcium *(mg)*	24.9
Phosphorus *(mg)*	103.4
Iron *(mg)*	1.2
Sodium *(mg)*	533.6
Zinc *(mg)*	0.9

Kesra

This home-made bread is commonly consumed throughout the Maghreb countries. It is made from flour usually extracted from hard-wheat varieties, but it can also be prepared from barley or corn flours. In Algeria, the preferred name for *kesra* is *mattoua*.

Preparation. Wheat flour is mixed with salted water and a small amount of dough retained from a previous batch (or with commercial yeast) and kneaded vigorously to obtain a firm dough. The dough is allowed to rise for one to two hours then divided into balls of approximately 250 g each. One ball is kept as a leaven for the next day's bread, and the rest is shaped into loaves about 20 cm in diameter and 2 cm thick. On certain occasions, the bread is sprinkled with sesame and anise seeds. Baking usually requires a

TABLE 7
Proximate gross composition of *kesra*
(value per 100 g edible portion)

Component	Value
Energy value *(kcal)*	255
Moisture *(g)*	35
Protein *(g)*	7
Lipids *(g)*	0.8
Carbohydrates *(g)*	55

few minutes, and the final product is a crispy bread with a well-browned crust and a thin crumb.

Today, wheat flour tends to be used more often for bread preparation, and commercial yeast tends also to replace leavening by sour dough.

Table 7 illustrates the nutritive value of kesra.

Kisra

This bread is the staple food of the Sudan. It is prepared from sorghum or millet flours. By far, however, the bulk of *kisra* is made from the various types of sorghum grown in rain-fed areas of the country.

The word kisra can be considered a generic name for a variety of breads and porridges formed from fermented sorghum dough; it is mostly used, however, to denote a special kind of bread baked in a special way in very thin sheets on a hot plate called *doka*.

Preparation. Sorghum flour is fermented by a simple, spontaneous process. Sorghum flour is traditionally milled using a stone mill or quern. In some cases the grains are first dehulled with a wooden mortar and pestle or a mechanical electric mill.

The flour is mixed with water and with a small portion of the previous lot of fermented sorghum dough as a starter. The dough is incubated in a warm corner of the house, covered and left to ferment overnight.

The fermentation of the dough was found to be mixed, with lactic-acid bacteria and acetic-acid bacteria playing the major role. Yeasts are found, but have a minor role. Lactic acid, acetic acid, butyric acid and a little ethanol are found in the fermented product, but lactic acid is by far the major one.

Fresh flour or water may be added to the dough after fermentation to adjust the consistency. Baking takes place on a hot plate, heated traditionally by burning wood or charcoal, or more recently, by electricity. The thickness of the baked sheet is 1-2 mm, and the hot plate is frequently coated with animal brain heated in bone marrow or sesame oil to prevent adherence of the bread to the hot plate. The batter is spread quickly in the form of a crescent using a thin wooden spatula. Baking time is about 30 seconds, and the baked sheet is removed by hand. The shelf-life of this bread is about one day.

Nutritive value. Fermentation of sorghum flour produces an increase in its crude protein content. The *Feterita* variety of sorghum shows a clear increase in the majority of amino-acids, while other varieties sometimes show a drop in some amino-acids. Lysine and methionine are little affected during fermentation.

The composition of kisra on average is: 14 percent protein, 1.5 percent ash, 2.5 percent crude fibre and 1.0 percent sugar, on dry matter basis. The moisture content of kisra sheets is about 50 percent.

Date bread

Date bread (*khoubez al-tamer*) is one of the traditional foods commonly consumed in the Arabian Gulf countries. It is baked in a special clay oven built in the ground. It is often consumed with the traditional sweet *halwa* (see p. 131) and Arabic coffee during weddings, religious ceremonies and other social occasions. Consumption of this kind of bread is on the decrease, and few local bakeries still produce it.

TABLE 8
Proximate gross composition and mineral content of date bread
(value per 100 g edible portion)

Component	Value
Energy value *(kcal)*	315
Moisture *(g)*	20.1
Protein *(g)*	7.7
Lipids *(g)*	1.7
Ash *(g)*	1
Crude fibre *(g)*	0.5
Carbohydrates *(g)*	69
Calcium *(mg)*	5.3
Phosphorus *(mg)*	–
Iron *(mg)*	1.8
Sodium *(mg)*	88.7
Zinc *(mg)*	6.6

Preparation. Wheat flour, dates and/or date syrup (*dibbs*), sugar, dry active yeast and water are the main ingredients used in the preparation of khoubez al-tamer. For preparation, the sugar is first dissolved in water, and then flour, dates and yeast are added. The ingredients are mixed well until a dough of good consistency has formed. The dough is then cut into pieces and flattened, and sometimes sesame seeds are spread over the surface before baking at 400°C in an earthenware oven until brown.

Nutritive value. This kind of bread is high in energy and minerals (see Table 8) compared with other breads, due to the inclusion of dates and date syrup in its formulation.

OTHER CEREAL-BASED FOODS
Kaak and kaak b'zaatar
This kind of bread is prepared in the form of a large flat hollow ring and has one surface covered with sesame seeds. Its flavour is usually more sour than that of regular bread; it is often consumed with ground thyme (*zaatar*) as a snack. It is usually sold by street vendors in Lebanon and the Syrian Arab Republic and to some extent in Jordan.

Preparation. A special chickpea steep liquor is used as a starter to prepare *kaak* by mixing the following ingredients:

Cracked chickpea	10 parts by weight
Water	100
Salt	1

The mixture is fermented overnight to form a broth as an indication of bacterial activity. The dough sheets are prepared as described earlier for Arabic bread, except that the liquor is used as the leavening agent, and sesame seeds are sprinkled on the surface of the dough before baking.

Nutritive value. Kaak is considered a rich source of food energy and has slightly better nutritive value than bread because of the protein contribution of the leavening agent and the sesame seeds (see Table 9).

Burghol
Burghol is commonly used in all countries of the Near East, but its preparation is mainly limited to the wheat-producing countries of the Near East and North Africa. Burghol is actually a parboiled wheat prepared from hard-wheat varieties. It is commonly consumed as a main dish combined with meat, tomatoes or a green salad rich in parsley leaves. It can also be used as a rice substitute for stuffing poultry.

Preparation. Wheat kernels are cleaned from chaff and dirt and then immersed in boiling water for two hours. This boiling step allows the hot water to penetrate into the seeds, dissolving with it some of the vitamins and minerals that are usually present in the outer bran layer of wheat seeds. As

TABLE 9
Proximate gross composition of *kaak*
(value per 100 g edible portion)

Component	Value
Energy value *(kcal)*	294
Moisture *(g)*	21.6
Protein *(g)*	10.4
Lipids *(g)*	1
Ash *(g)*	1.8
Crude fibre *(g)*	0.8
Nitrogen-free extract *(g)*	64.4

the water soaks into the endosperm, it carries with it the solubilized nutrients to the inside of the grain. The hot water also causes gelatinization of the starch granules and kills the germs and insect eggs that may be present. The wheat seeds are then removed from the hot-water soak and spread in the sun until completely dry. The dried seeds are tempered to a low moisture content by sprinkling them with a light spray of water. This water is quickly absorbed by the outer bran layers, which change from brittle to tough, leathery and easy to remove by hand rubbing or by mechanical abrasion. The peeled grains are spread again in the sun until completely dry. They are then ground into coarse particles that are separated according to size into fine or coarse grades.

The final product may have a long shelf-life if strict hygiene is maintained after the boiling step. Grading and packing of burghol can facilitate its use, improve its appearance and increase its acceptability by the consumer.

Nutritive value. Burghol is considered a good source of easily digested carbohydrates, superior to wheat in this regard. For its composition, see Table 10.

TABLE 10
Proximate gross composition of *burghol*
(value per 100 g edible portion)

Component	Value
Energy value *(kcal)*	353
Moisture *(g)*	7.5
Protein *(g)*	12.2
Lipids *(g)*	2.3
Ash *(g)*	1.2
Carbohydrates *(g)*	74.9

Melthuth and *tchicha*

This food is made from barley and is consumed mainly by rural populations in areas of the Maghreb countries where this cereal is produced. It is actually a roasted barley ground into gross particles and steamed like couscous and dried in the sun. It is less frequently consumed than couscous, and its consumption is mainly limited to the month of Ramadan.

Preparation. The barley kernels are separated from chaff and roasted in an earthenware pan (*tajin*) until brown. The roasting of cereals causes a partial gelatinization of the starch granules, kills the germs and insect eggs that may be present, reduces the moisture content of the grains and enhances their digestibility. The grains are then peeled and winnowed or sifted to remove the envelopes that constitute the outer bran layers. The peeled grains are then ground and sieved to separate the coarse particles or *melthuth*. A second sieving with a narrow-mesh sieve retains a finer grade or *tchicha*, while a flour-like product passes through. Melthuth/tchicha and barley flour are stored for winter and spring consumption.

Melthuth is consumed steamed, like couscous (see p. 19), with accompanying sauces. It is also eaten with lamb's head and feet. Tchicha, on

TABLE 11
Proximate gross composition of *melthuth* and *tchicha*
(value per 100 g edible portion)

Component	Value
Energy value *(kcal)*	359
Moisture *(g)*	11.4
Protein *(g)*	8.8
Lipids *(g)*	1
Carbohydrates *(g)*	78.8

the other hand, is consumed as a soup prepared with vegetables alone, or vegetables mixed with meat or fish. The latter is often consumed during the month of Ramadan.

The keeping quality of melthuth and tchicha may be enhanced if fresh barley is used and if strict hygiene is maintained during the peeling, grinding and sifting steps. Storage should take place in a dry atmosphere. Industrial processing and packaging of melthuth and tchicha will increase consumer acceptance, reduce risk of contamination and most important increase their availability to urban consumers. A national firm specialized in the trituration of barley is producing these products on an industrial scale in the Republic of Tunisia. There is, however, a large scope for improving the keeping quality and the commercial aspects of the product.

Table 11 illustrates the nutritive value of melthuth and tchicha.

Freekeh or fereek
This food is commonly prepared from the immature grains of durum wheat at the milky stage. Soft-wheat varieties may also be used. It is very popular in many countries of the Near East, particularly Jordan, Syria and Egypt. It is commonly consumed as a main dish combined with meat or with tomato sauce or as a stuffing for poultry.

Preparation. *Freekeh* is still prepared manually, although there are some efforts in Jordan to mechanize and standardize the manufacturing procedure. The stage at which wheat is harvested for freekeh preparation is very critical; the preferred moment is when the leaves start turning yellow and the seeds are still soft and creamy. The harvested wheat is arranged in small piles and placed in the sun for 24 hours to partially dry. The piles are then set on fire, and the progress of the blaze is carefully controlled to burn the straw and chaff but not the seeds. The high moisture content of the seeds prevents them from catching fire. The location of the burning site, prevailing wind and close supervision help in making the effects of burning on flavour, texture and colour as uniform as possible. The roasted wheat is then subjected to further drying in the sun before thrashing. The seeds are collected and spread in a shady place for final dehydration to a moisture content of about 9 percent. The freekeh seeds are then cracked by a special mill into smaller pieces like burghol (see p. 13) and generally used in cooking instead of rice.

The seeds have a dark greenish colour and impart to foods a smoked flavour. The resulting food has a distinct flavour that develops during burning and dehydration.

Nutritive value. Since freekeh is mostly used as a substitute for rice, its production and consumption must be encouraged for the following reasons.
- Freekeh has much better nutritive value than rice because of its higher protein, vitamin and mineral contents (see Table 12).
- Freekeh comes from a plant that is well adapted to the region and can be grown locally quite successfully. Rice has to be imported to most countries of the Near East.

Mirmiz or frik

Mirmiz, or barley *frik,* is made from immature barley grains and used for the preparation of soups. It is actually a parboiled (or steamed) and dried barley. In the past, its consumption was almost exclusively limited to the barley-producing rural areas of North Africa. Currently, it is also consumed in many cities of the Maghreb countries.

TABLE 12
Proximate gross composition of *freekeh*
(value per 100 g edible portion)

Component	Value
Energy value *(kcal)*	391
Moisture *(g)*	9.5
Protein *(g)*	13
Lipids *(g)*	2
Ash *(g)*	1.8
Carbohydrates *(g)*	70

Preparation. Barley is mowed and thrashed before full maturation of the grains. In addition to their low bran content, the immature grains give a special taste to the final product. These grains are mixed with salt and boiled which makes the husk more easily detachable, renders the grains less brittle and more elastic and toughens the outside of the barley grain by a process of starch gelatinization. Soon after boiling, the grains are spread out to dry in the sun for one or two days, then peeled in a mortar to detach the outer bran layers. The peeled grains are slightly roasted in an earthenware pan. This operation enhances the rapid preparation time which characterizes the product, kills contaminating germs and reduces moisture content, thus enhancing its storage life. After roasting, the grains are ground and sieved to produce three different fractions:
- the coarse particles are used to prepare couscous;
- the flour that passes through the sieve is used to prepare *bsissa*, a cereal pap (see p. 29);
- the medium-size particles constitute the mirmiz or frik, which is used in the preparation of soups.

The same process can be applied to immature grains of wheat. The product obtained is then called frik; the word mirmiz is limited to barley only.

This product is becoming increasingly popular, and its consumption is on the rise. It also has a good potential for industrial production, while its long and complex processing inhibits its preparation at home. This product is

TABLE 13
Proximate gross composition of *mirmiz* or *frik*
(value per 100 g edible portion)

Component	Value
Energy value *(kcal)*	337
Moisture *(g)*	11.5
Protein *(g)*	10.7
Lipids *(g)*	1.6
Carbohydrates *(g)*	76.2

currently produced on a cottage scale and marketed in commercial outlets, particularly by street vendors.

There is a large scope for improving the hygienic and keeping qualities of this product as well as its consumer acceptance through better processing of the raw material and improved handling and packaging of the final product.

For its nutritive value, see Table 13.

Couscous

The ancient inhabitants of the Maghreb are probably the first people who used the steaming technique for cooking barley and wheat semolina. Couscous preparation follows well-defined processing steps that have direct physical, biochemical and nutritional effects on the product. Today, couscous is a very common traditional food consumed by almost all the families in the Maghreb countries at least once a week. The Berber designation for this food is *sekrou*, while it is known as *maftoul* or *moghrabiyyeh* in the countries of the east Mediterranean and *suksukaniyyah* in the Sudan. In the Kingdom of Morocco, it is sometimes made from corn instead of wheat.

Preparation. Couscous is essentially prepared from durum wheat, but in certain barley-growing areas barley or a mixture of barley and wheat can also be used. To prepare couscous, two grades of semolina are required: fine and coarse. The coarse grains serve as a nucleus that fixes the fine particles to form the typical couscous grains. First, coarse semolina is sprinkled with water and a little salt and stirred by hand to get a uniform distribution of moisture. The fine semolina is sprinkled with one hand while the other hand stirs and rolls. Rolling is continued with the palm of the right hand, while water and fine semolina are alternately added until the grains agglomerate to the desired size. The grains are then calibrated through a sieve to obtain a product of homogeneous particle size, which undergoes uniform cooking during the steaming step.

Couscous can be prepared for immediate consumption or it can be stored. To be preserved, couscous should be first precooked by steaming with boiling water. This operation is done with a special cooking device, or couscous cooker (*keskès*), composed of two parts: a cooking pan for broth or boiling water and a steamer. When the water comes to a boil, the couscous is poured in the steamer and kept there for 30-40 minutes. The grains are then sprinkled with fresh water and stirred with a large wooden spoon both to break the lumps of particles that have formed during steaming and to aerate the grains of couscous.

The couscous is then spread on a cloth and sundried for three to four days. When it is completely dry, couscous is stored in large containers and placed in a dry storeroom.

In certain areas of the country, the steaming step can be bypassed, and the grains of couscous, prepared in the same way described above, are sundried and then stored. This type of couscous needs two cycles of steaming during the final cooking to compensate for the first one.

In the preparation of couscous, three processing steps have a great effect on the physical, biochemical and nutritive properties of the final product. First, the texture of couscous and its composition are improved compared to the composition of the grain. It was shown that in making couscous, elements of the grain are reconstituted but the internal order is reversed. The digestibility of the particles always improves and is higher than that of the

TABLE 14
Proximate gross composition of couscous
(value per 100 g edible portion)

Component	Value
Energy value *(kcal)*	350
Moisture *(g)*	13.2
Protein *(g)*	12
Lipids *(g)*	1.1
Ash *(g)*	1.2
Carbohydrates *(g)*	75

sticky and compact textures found in paps, porridges and breads. Second, steaming brings about a partial gelatinization of starch, which also improves its digestibility. Finally, drying reduces the water content of the product and has a direct effect on its keeping quality. For its nutritive value, see Table 14.

To improve the quality and shelf-life of couscous, these three steps should be properly executed. The quality of couscous also depends on the type of wheat grains, the grades of semolina and the quality of water used during the mixing and rolling steps. Strict hygiene during drying and storing steps is very critical to the keeping quality of the final product.

Industrially precooked couscous is now commercialized on a large scale.

Mhammas

Like couscous, *mhammas* is made from hard-wheat varieties, but the grains are larger and their preparation is slightly different in that drying is much longer. Mhammas is prepared in all the Maghreb countries, and its consumption is more frequent during periods of cold weather. The Berber equivalent of this food is *timhamast*.

Preparation. In the initial stages of preparation, mhammas is manufactured, like couscous, by rolling coarse particles of semolina with a finer grade to

TABLE 15
Proximate gross composition of *mhammas*
(value per 100 g edible portion)

Component	Value
Energy value *(kcal)*	352
Moisture *(g)*	12.1
Protein *(g)*	14.3
Lipids *(g)*	2.7
Carbohydrates *(g)*	70.9

form grains of approximately twice the size of those used for the preparation of couscous. To obtain grains of uniform size, sifting is necessary. The grains are then spread in the sun for five to seven days until completely dry. After that, the grains are rolled again with slices of onions and salted water. The rolling step takes one to two days until the grains become smooth, glossy and homogeneous. The grains of mhammas are spread again in the sun for seven to ten days until completely dry. As with couscous, mhammas is then left in a room for one or two days to allow the grains to reach the moisture level of the room. It is believed that the mhammas should not be stored immediately after drying, because an increase in volume is expected after absorption of ambient moisture.

Like couscous, the final product may have a long shelf-life if sufficiently dried before storage in a dry atmosphere, and if strict hygiene is maintained during the processing steps. Industrially prepared mhammas may be properly packaged and made available to consumers at a relatively low cost.

Mhammas can be cooked in different ways. A simple preparation is obtained with a tomato sauce to which vegetables are also added.

For its nutritive value, see Table 15.

Saykouk

Saykouk is a steamed couscous prepared from barley and then buttered and soaked in buttermilk. It is frequently consumed in the Maghreb countries during summer as an accompanying food to a principal meal or as a mid-day snack. It is greatly appreciated by consumers for its refreshing and cooling properties during the hot season.

Preparation. Couscous is prepared in the classical way described earlier (see p. 20), with the difference that barley is used instead of wheat. The cereal is ground and then sieved to remove the bran and to separate three products for different uses. One of these products, made of the coarse fraction, serves to prepare saykouk. This product is sprinkled with water, rolled by hand in a large plate and carefully dropped in a steamer for 15-20 minutes. When the steam passes through, the couscous is removed, slightly watered, rolled again to aerate the grains and put back on the steamer for a second steaming. After another 15-20 minutes, the couscous is buttered and soaked in buttermilk.

As for couscous, steaming plays an important role in the preparation of saykouk. It increases the digestibility of the product and enhances its acceptability. The addition of butter and buttermilk results in a final product with high nutritive value. However, the preparation of the raw ingredient is complex and time consuming. It must be produced on a commercial scale if its consumption is to be increased.

Table 16 illustrates the nutritive value of saykouk.

Hlalim

Hlalim is a fermented and dried pasta made from hard-wheat varieties. It serves as a cereal base for a soup prepared with a variety of legumes. This hot soup is commonly used in winter in several Maghreb countries.

Preparation. Fine wheat semolina is kneaded with warm water, salt and leavened bread to make a firm dough. The dough is covered with a piece of cloth and left in a warm place to ferment for two to three hours. The next step is an elaborate processing of the dough into small pieces. A piece of dough,

TABLE 16
Proximate gross composition of *saykouk*
(value per 100 g edible portion)

Component	Value
Energy value *(kcal)*	85.9
Moisture *(g)*	80.7
Protein *(g)*	3.1
Lipids *(g)*	1.7
Carbohydrates *(g)*	14.5

about the size of an egg, is rolled between the palms of the hands, stretched into a fine thread and, with the thumb and forefinger, the thread is regularly cut into pieces 1 cm long. The pieces fall side to side on the back of a sieve. When the sieve is fully covered, it is taken to dry in the sun, and the operation is continued until the dough is used up. Drying takes about one to two days.

Hlalim constitutes the cereal component of a soup that is largely consumed during winter. The soup is usually prepared with a traditionally preserved meat called *kadide*, which gives an additional aroma to this appetizing dish. The inclusion of legumes (chickpeas, broad beans and white beans) and vegetables (onion, parsley, celery and green peas) in its preparation makes it a highly nutritious and inexpensive food.

The fermentation process gives a special taste and texture to the pasta that is specific to this product. Hlalim is currently produced on family scale and marketed by street vendors. There is a large scope for improving the fermentation, handling and marketing of this product. Strict hygiene should be maintained after fermentation. Given its potential for industrial production and commercialization, proper packaging is needed to improve storage time and consumer acceptance.

Table 17 depicts the composition of hlalim.

TABLE 17
Proximate gross composition of hlalim
(value per 100 g edible portion)

Component	Value
Energy value *(kcal)*	340
Moisture *(g)*	11.6
Protein *(g)*	13.2
Lipids *(g)*	1.1
Nitrogen-free extract *(g)*	74.1

Ftaier

Ftaier, as known in Tunisia, are fermented and deep-fried fritters made from wheat flour and consumed at breakfast or as midday snacks. In Algeria and Morocco, they are known as *sfenj*. They used to be prepared at home on a regular basis, but their domestic preparation has significantly declined; they are now prepared by street vendors regularly. These fritters can be eaten plain, or soaked in a heavy sugar syrup.

Preparation. About 500 g of wheat flour is moistened with warm water and mixed with a small quantity of leaven. Some olive oil and an egg are added and left to ferment for two hours. The fermented paste is then divided into small pieces of 60-100 g each and impregnated with oil. The dough pieces are then stretched and rounded to a circular shape and thrown into the middle of a large frying pan for deep-frying. After one or two minutes, the fritters are removed from the frying pan and the oil drained before consumption.

Nutritive value. Burnet and Viscontini have measured the nutrient content of plain fritters without the addition of eggs. An approximation was made by the author to include one egg in a 600-g portion of uncooked paste made by using 250 g of wheat flour (see Table 18). This quantity serves to prepare an average of ten fritters.

TABLE 18
Proximate gross composition of ftaier
(value per 100 g edible portion)

Component	Value
Energy value *(kcal)*	410
Moisture *(g)*	28
Protein *(g)*	6.3
Lipids *(g)*	27.5
Ash *(g)*	1.4
Carbohydrates *(g)*	34.4

Uhbik

A Berber word meaning the first meal of the day, *uhbik* is usually made from raw cereal flour mixed with olive oil and eaten with dried figs and barley *kesra*. Uhbik can actually be made of barley, wheat, maize, broad beans, green peas or lentils. Its processing is very simple and involves pounding the selected ingredient and mixing it with olive oil.

Preparation. Barley and wheat flour are the basic cereals used to prepare this breakfast food. Grains of barley or wheat are ground between heavy granite stones and sieved to separate bran and gross particles. A second grinding results in a floury product that is stored to prepare uhbik. Uhbik is prepared for consumption by mixing such flour with olive oil and a pinch of salt. It can also be stored in the shape of a loaf of bread and taken as food-supply by shepherds and travellers. Uhbik does not undergo any cooking and thus is not subject to any biochemical or nutritive transformation. Berbers in North Africa, however, attribute special nutritive and therapeutic qualities to it.

Another category of uhbik is made with legumes. Legumes used are broad beans, green peas or lentils. The processing follows the same simple steps described above, except that the legumes are roasted before they are ground

TABLE 19
Proximate gross composition of *uhbik*
(value per 100 g edible portion)

Component	Value
Energy value *(kcal)*	391
Moisture *(g)*	8.7
Protein *(g)*	12
Lipids *(g)*	12.5
Ash *(g)*	3.1
Carbohydrates *(g)*	63.6

and then added to the barley and wheat-flour milk. Roasting has direct physical, biochemical and nutritional effects on the final product. It particularly improves the digestibility, safety and keeping quality of the product. Uhbik made of a mixture of cereals and legumes after roasting is recommended for large-scale production.

Nutritive value. The addition of oil to the flour mixture causes this food to be relatively high in food calories. Table 19 shows its composition.

Rghaief

Rghaief in the Maghreb countries refers to an unleavened bread made from wheat flour with a filling consisting of animal fat, red pepper, onions and various spices. Rghaief is known as *mlawi* or *rqaiq* in Tunisia and as *arghum* in Algeria. They are commonly consumed in the city of Fes with tea to accompany breakfast.

Preparation. *Rghaief* has a cereal outer coat and a filling component. The cereal component is made of a dough softer than that for bread but less liquid than that for fritters. To obtain the dough, wheat flour is mixed with water

TABLE 20
Proximate gross composition of *rhgaief*
(value per 100 g edible portion)

Component	Value
Energy value *(kcal)*	254
Moisture *(g)*	61.9
Protein *(g)*	3.1
Lipids *(g)*	21
Carbohydrates *(g)*	14

than that for fritters. To obtain the dough, wheat flour is mixed with water and salt and kneaded for half an hour until it develops a rubbery consistency. The elasticity of the dough is very important to obtain pastry layers. It is thus necessary that the batter should not undergo any fermentation. When sufficiently kneaded, the dough is divided into small balls, the size of an egg. The balls are then flattened into layers 1.5 cm thick and 20 x 40 cm for other dimensions. By the time the pastry layers are completed, the filling should be ready. One type of filling is made with traditional preserved fat called *lakhliâa* (see p. 86) to which onions are added in slices. Another filling can be specially prepared with lamb or beef fats. Fats are cut into fine pieces or ground and mixed with crushed pepper, chopped onion, parsley and ground cumin. These ingredients are cooked over a low heat until the fats are completely melted. The filling is then thinly spread on one third of the pastry layer, which is rolled into a cylindrical shape and flattened. The product is then baked or fried in a greasy pan rubbed with onions.

Table 20 illustrates the nutritive value of rghaief.

Shâariya

Shâariya is a pasta made from hard-wheat semolina. The processing is simple and involves kneading, shaping and sundrying. The noodles are used

TABLE 21
Proximate gross composition of *shâariya*
(value per 100 g edible portion)

Component	Value
Energy value *(kcal)*	352
Moisture *(g)*	12.1
Protein *(g)*	14.3
Lipids *(g)*	2.7
Carbohydrates *(g)*	70.9

cinnamon and cold milk. Shâariya is commonly eaten in Tunisia and some other Maghreb countries.

Preparation. Fine semolina from hard-wheat varieties is sprinkled with salted water and kneaded to form a dough with the same consistency as that for bread. The dough is then allowed to rest for several hours. Then, between the thumb and the forefinger, a small quantity of dough is rolled in the form of spaghetti, 1 cm long. The formed pieces are then spread in the sun to dry. The final product, which looks like vermicelli, may be used immediately or can be stored for later consumption. Shâariya is prepared at home but has the potential to be processed on a larger scale and made available to a large number of consumers.

Nutritive value. Specific data are not available. The following values are generated from appropriate food-composition tables (see Table 21).

FOODS BASED ON CEREAL-LEGUME MIXTURES
Bsissa

Bsissa, as it is known in Tunisia, is prepared from cereals alone, such as barley or wheat, or a mixture of cereals and legumes. The grains are roasted and mixed with carrot powder or with sugar and olive oil. Largely consumed as a breakfast food by the rural sector of the population, it can also be the sole source of nourishment a shepherd or traveller may have for a few days. In Algeria, it is called *tabsist*.

Preparation. Wheat or barley kernels are cleaned from chaff and dirt and roasted in a large earthenware pan. Spices such as coriander, cumin and fennel or anise seeds are also roasted with the cereals. While barley is used alone in the preparation of bsissa, wheat is often mixed with two or three pulses: chickpeas, broad beans and fenugreek. The roasted grains are then finely ground and sieved. Only the flour is retained to prepare bsissa. Bsissa can be stored as flour or in ready-to-eat form. In the latter case, bsissa is mixed with olive oil and sugar.

The roasting of the cereal grains and pulses serves many purposes. It improves the aroma of the food mixture and hence increases its acceptability by the consumer; it also kills contaminating germs and reduces the moisture content, thus increasing the shelf-life of the final product. As a pre-cooking step, roasting has a viscosity-reducing effect on cereals and pulses that improves their dietary bulk. Because of these properties, bsissa is considered suitable for infants and young children.

Bsissa is at present an exclusively home-made food. However, the availability of its ingredients, the relative ease of its preparation, its high nutritive value (see Table 22) and its good keeping properties confer to it a great potential for industrial production.

Mode of consumption

Bsissa from barley. The most popular way of consuming bsissa is a drink made with bsissa flour and flavoured with spices such as coriander, cumin, anise seeds and fenugreek. This drink sweetened with sugar is highly appreciated during summer for its thirst-quenching and refreshing qualities. It is usually consumed as a breakfast drink.

Bsissa from wheat. Bsissa from wheat is usually mixed with chickpeas, broad beans and fenugreek seeds in addition to the usual spices. All the ingredients are roasted, ground into fine flour and mixed with olive oil and sugar to the desired taste. Other ingredients can be added: almonds, nuts,

TABLE 22
Proximate gross composition of *bsissa*
(value per 100 g, wet-weight basis)

Component	Bsissa Mixture of wheat and pulses	With sugar and oil
Energy value *(kcal)*	363	450
Moisture *(g)*	7	11
Protein *(g)*	18.5	8.8
Lipids *(g)*	18.5	23
Carbohydrates *(g)*	55.8	57.2

sugar to the desired taste. Other ingredients can be added: almonds, nuts, Syrian halwa, dates, etc. This type of bsissa is usually consumed at breakfast or taken as a food snack by travellers and shepherds.

Assidat homs
This type of *assidat* is made of two parts of roasted wheat and one part of roasted chickpeas. This food mixture is prepared as a special weaning food in northern Tunisia (Kelibia) as well as in other parts of the country.

Preparation. As for bsissa, the kernels of hard wheat are slightly roasted, ground and sieved to remove bran and parts of the germ. Chickpeas are roasted separately, ground and then sieved to separate and collect the fine flour. A mixture of two parts of wheat and one part of chickpea flour constitutes the basic ingredients that make assidat homs. Roasting plays a major role in enhancing the acceptability, digestibility and keeping quality of the food. It also reduces the hot-paste consistency of the food, making it particularly suitable for infant feeding.

Commercially marketed semolina can be roasted and used instead of roasted wheat, thus facilitating the preparation significantly.

TABLE 23
Proximate gross composition of *assidat homs*
(value per 100 g edible portion)

Component	Value
Energy value *(kcal)*	420
Moisture *(g)*	9.8
Protein *(g)*	15.7
Lipids *(g)*	3
Carbohydrates *(g)*	71.5

Nutritive value. Assidat homs can be an excellent weaning food, since it is a good source of proteins and carbohydrates. Its composition is illustrated in Table 23.

Koshary and *mjaddarah*

Koshary is the Egyptian name of a food prepared in many countries of North Africa from a mixture of lentils and rice usually in the proportion of 1:2 (w/w). In many other Near Eastern countries, such as Lebanon, the Syrian Arab Republic and Jordan, the food is known as *mjaddarah*, and the amount of rice is minimal, about 10-20 percent of the weight of the lentils.

Preparation. Koshary is prepared in different ways, the simplest of which (plain koshary) is to cook a mixture of rice and lentils, previously sorted and washed, in an equal weight of water. Ghee may be added either to the boiling water or used for lightly frying the dry mixture before cooking. Salt and spices are added during or after cooking. The cooking procedure is usually carried out in two stages; in the first, the mixture is allowed to boil till most of the free water is evaporated. The heat is then reduced considerably until the cooking process is completed.

Instant koshary is made by steeping lentils and rice grains in water at 25°C for about two hours, followed by boiling for ten minutes. The mixture is then dehydrated in a drying cabinet, initially at 200°C for three minutes and then

TABLE 24
Proximate gross composition and mineral content of *koshary*
(value per 100 g edible portion)

Component	Value
Energy value *(kcal)*	401
Protein *(g)*	16
Lipids *(crude ether extract) (g)*	1
Ash *(g)*	1.2
Crude fibre *(g)*	0.4
Carbohydrates *(g)*	82
Calcium *(mg)*	1.6
Phosphorus *(mg)*	22
Iron *(mg)*	0.2
Potassium *(mg)*	17

at 100°C for six hours. After dehydration, it is packed in polyethylene bags and sealed. This product has a long shelf-life at room temperature. For domestic consumption, instant koshary is rehydrated and cooked in an equal weight of water for six minutes. Industrial production is still in its initial stages.

Nutritive value. Lentils are rich in protein (23 percent), but their protein is 25 percent deficient in tryptophan and sulphur-containing amino-acids. The protein content of rice is low (8 percent), but it is of good quality and rich in sulphur-containing amino-acids. By blending rice and lentils, digestibility is improved and the relative distribution of amino-acids is modified. Thus a lentil-rice mixture in the proportion of 1:2 improves the protein quality over that of either lentils or rice alone. Potassium and phosphorus constitute the major minerals in the ash of koshary; it was found that prolonged steeping prior to cooking may reduce considerably the ash content of this food. For its composition, see Table 24.

LEGUME FOODS
Foul mdammas

Foul mdammas is a very popular food made from one type of legume, the fava bean. Most often eaten at breakfast, it is heavily consumed in Egypt, but widely accepted in all other countries of the Near East. In North Africa, it is usually consumed as a soup, mixed with pieces of bread and spiced with cumin and *harissa* (a hot chilli paste). Nutritionally, it constitutes a meal by itself, especially if it receives additional protein supplements. Some people of the area suffer from a hereditary disease called favism, and such individuals cannot tolerate the consumption of fava beans.

Preparation. The fava beans, sometimes referred to as broad beans, are washed and soaked overnight in cold water. The soaking water is sometimes made 2-3 percent in sodium bicarbonate to soften the seed coat and facilitate cooking, resulting in more tender beans. The soaking solution, which is usually five times the weight of the dry beans, is salted to a final sodium-chloride concentration of 2 percent, and the mixture is stewed gently for six hours. The cooked beans are prepared for consumption by adding mashed garlic, lemon juice and some olive oil.

The cooking quality of beans varies greatly according to variety, post-harvest handling, storage period and stewing procedures. Home-made mdammas is usually stewed in special containers or in pressure cookers. Mdammas as prepared in restaurants and by street vendors is stewed in big jars over a low fire for long periods of time. Oil and salt are usually added to mdammas dishes.

For export and intracountry trade purposes, mdammas is also canned by big canneries in Egypt, Jordan, Lebanon, the Sudan and the Syrian Arab Republic. Two procedures are adopted for can processing. According to the first procedure, cleaned and sorted beans are steeped in water for four to 12 hours, depending on the size of the beans and the steeping temperature. The beans are then sorted again, washed and blanched for 30 minutes at 82°C and cooled. The beans are then packed in cans in a proportion of 33-35 percent of the net weight of the can. The packing solution is then added hot (82°C) in a proportion of 64.95-66.95 percent of the net weight of the can, followed by the addition of oil in a proportion of 0.05 percent. The cans are then exhausted at 88°C for ten minutes, double-seamed and sterilized at 115°C for 3 1/2 - 4 1/2 hours, depending on can size and bean variety. The cans are then cooled, labelled, arranged in carton cases and stored for about two weeks before they are sorted and marketed. The packing solution consists of 5 percent lentils or lentil soup, 1.5 percent salt, 1.25 percent tomato paste and 0.25 percent citric acid. The solution is strained hot and then heated to 82°C just before filling the cans.

According to the second procedure, cleaned and sorted beans are steeped for 18 hours and then precooked for 15 minutes at 90°C, cooled and packed to 50 percent of can capacity. Oil is then added in a proportion of 1 percent of can capacity, and the cans are filled with brine solution (1.7 percent) acidified with 0.7 percent citric acid (at 60°C) and then double-seamed. They are then sterilized and cooked in retorts at three stages; precooking for 35 minutes at 60°C, followed by cooking for 35 minutes at 125°C, then cooling to 36-40°C. By the time the cans reach the labelling machine, their outer surface is quite dry. They are then labelled, arranged in carton cases and stored for about two weeks before they are sorted and marketed. Such cans have a shelf-life of at least two years.

Nutritive value. Vicia faba is the most important member of the Leguminosae family because it is widely used as a protein-rich food and a major ingredient in several popular traditional foods. Legume proteins are in general rich in lysine but deficient in sulphur-containing amino-acids. Legumes in general contain trypsin inhibitors, which decrease digestibility of the food if consumed uncooked. This unhealthy effect is eliminated during processing and cooking. Processed fava beans are considered a good source of phosphorous, iron, copper and potassium, although about one third of the potassium content is lost during cooking. Mdammas was reported to have the composition depicted in Table 25.

TABLE 25
Proximate gross composition of *foul mdammas*
(value per 100 g edible portion)

Component	Value
Energy value *(kcal)*	424
Protein *(g)*	27
Lipids *(crude ether extract) (g)*	14
Crude fibre *(g)*	7
Carbohydrates *(g)*	47

Leblebi

Legume soup, or *leblebi*, is a well-known, traditional food made of steeped, slightly fermented and boiled legumes, such as chickpeas, broad beans and lentils. The legumes are mixed with bread, harissa, olive oil and various spices. The consumption of these soups is very common in winter at breakfast or as a midday snack. Leblebi is the most popular legume soup in the Maghreb countries and is mainly based on chickpeas.

Preparation. Chickpeas are sorted, cleaned and soaked overnight in water. This soaking may involve a partial overnight fermentation. Very often baking soda (sodium bicarbonate) is added to soften the grains. Baking soda is known to improve the texture, taste and cooking quality of chickpeas. The seeds are usually washed with fresh water and boiled for two to three hours with salt and a little olive oil. After cooking, the watery soup is generously poured on stale bread cut into fine pieces. The bread absorbs the broth and increases in volume. Cumin, salt and harissa are sprinkled on the top and mixed thoroughly to give the thick pasty soup an attractive red colour. A spoonful of vinegar or lemon juice adds acidity to the hot and spicy odours, resulting in the typical flavour of leblebi.

Leblebi used to be a home-prepared food. It is now offered in small restaurants and by most street vendors. Several other ingredients have

TABLE 26
Proximate gross composition of *leblebi*
(value per 100 g edible portion)

Component	Value
Energy value *(kcal)*	177
Moisture *(g)*	63.9
Protein *(g)*	6.1
Lipids *(crude ether extract)* *(g)*	5.6
Carbohydrates *(g)*	24.4

been incorporated in the basic recipe, such as boiled eggs, tuna fish and pickles.

Because of its high nutritive value and its microbiological safety due to the long boiling step, leblebi has a large potential for improvement. The long time it takes to cook leblebi (overnight soaking followed by two to three hours cooking) prevents this food from frequent consumption despite its nutritious quality and low cost. Manufacture of canned leblebi or dry instant mixes could greatly increase its consumption, particularly within the urban sector of the population.

Data on the nutritive value of leblebi were generated from various sources and are depicted in Table 26.

Bisara

Bisara is common to many countries in North Africa and is basically a cooked and minced suspension of fava beans spiced with a garlic-coriander mixture.

Preparation. According to the traditional methods for the preparation of bisara, the sorted, cleaned and decorticated fava beans are boiled for about one hour in three times their weight in water till they acquire a soft texture. Some garlic, green onions, coriander, green dill and peppermint leaves are added. The mixture is then minced, and ground cumin seeds, ground

TABLE 27
Proximate gross composition and mineral content of *bisara*
(value per 100 g edible portion)

Component	Value
Energy value *(kcal)*	183
Protein *(g)*	29
Lipids *(crude ether extract) (g)*	6
Ash *(g)*	8
Crude fibre *(g)*	3
Carbohydrates *(g)*	53
Calcium *(mg)*	84
Phosphorous *(mg)*	435
Iron *(mg)*	10
Potassium *(mg)*	1 670
Magnesium *(mg)*	190
Zinc *(mg)*	3

caraway seeds, dried peppermint leaves and salt are added. The mixture is boiled again, until it acquires a thick consistency. In the meantime chopped, ground or cut onions are fried in ghee till golden yellow in colour. A mixture of ground garlic and powdered coriander seeds are then added, and the whole mixture is fried. Half of the fried garlic-coriander mixture is then added to the cooked beans and stirred. The mixture is distributed into suitable dishes, and the surface is decorated by the rest of the fried garlic-coriander mixture.

Nutritive value. Bisara is a high-protein food that is easily digestible, and its consumption should be encouraged. Its proximate composition is depicted in Table 27.

Falafel

Falafel is an extremely popular legume-based food that is highly nutritious and rich in food energy. It can be conveniently consumed in the form of sandwiches, but has not lent itself to industrial processing in the form of a ready-to-eat food. In Egypt, it is prepared from fava beans only; in other countries of the Near East, it is prepared from a 2:1 mixture of fava beans and chickpeas.

Preparation. Falafel is prepared by first decorticating sorted and cleaned fava beans. The beans are then soaked in about three times their weight in water for about 16 hours at room temperature. The water is then drained and the softened cotyledons are mashed into a fine paste. Salt, spices and green onions are usually added during the mashing process. The resulting paste is usually left at room temperature for about 30 minutes to ferment. Portions of about 15 g each are then manually formed into balls and deep fried in oil (usually cottonseed oil) at about 175°C for about six minutes. The falafel balls may also be formed using a special scoop.

At the experimental level, falafel in the form of raw paste is packed in polyethylene bags and frozen. Such semi-processed frozen paste is very popular and generates a high demand for domestic consumption. Dehydrated falafel mixture is also prepared commercially. Such a mixture is composed of 85 percent of ground, decorticated beans and 15 percent spices and dehydrated green vegetables. For the preparation of such a product, decorticated beans are washed with water and dried by spreading them in the open air or in a hot air dryer. Dried decorticated beans are then mixed with dried spices, dried green vegetables and about 1-1.2 percent sodium bicarbonate. The mixture is ground and sieved using a 2-mm-mesh sieve, packed in polyethylene bags, and sealed and placed in small rectangular boxes. For rehydration, the dried mixture is thoroughly mixed with an equal weight of water and left for 20 minutes before it is ready for frying.

Nutritive value. Falafel combines the high protein content of fava beans and the rich amount of calories contributed by deep fat frying. It is a meal by itself, specially if supplemented with a food rich in methionine. Table 28 illustrates its composition.

TABLE 28
Proximate gross composition of *falafel*
(value per 100 g edible portion)

Component	Value
Energy value *(kcal)*	507
Protein *(g)*	24
Lipids *(crude ether extract) (g)*	32
Ash *(g)*	4
Crude fibre *(g)*	8
Carbohydrates *(g)*	32

Hommos b'tehineh

A very popular food in Lebanon, the Syrian Arab Republic, Jordan, Iraq and some of the Gulf countries, *hommos b'tehineh* is a chickpea dip commonly consumed as such or as an independent dish by itself. This food has been processed on an industrial scale and is produced in Lebanon and Jordan.

Preparation. The main ingredient in this food is chickpeas. The chickpeas have to be mashed to a very fine and smooth consistency. To accomplish this, whole chickpeas have to be softened by prolonged soaking in water, usually for a period of 12 hours or more. About 1 percent sodium bicarbonate is added to the soaking water to ensure softening of the chickpea seeds. The softened seeds are then boiled in 2 percent brine until soft and then passed through a mill or mashed in a heavy-duty, high-speed blender. Tehineh (for a description of tehineh see p. 146) is then added to the chickpeas during the pulverization process. The amount of tehineh used is usually half the weight of the chickpeas. Some lemon juice is then added to the mixture while blending. Citric acid can be used to replace the lemon juice either partially or totally. In commercial preparations, garlic is not added because its flavour changes during the heating step that follows, but in home preparations ground garlic is added at a rate of 15 percent of the weight of the chickpeas.

The final product has a smooth, viscous, semi-solid consistency, and is filled into 120-g tin cans and heated under pressure in a retort at 121°C for one hour. Larger cans require longer cooking periods, because heat penetration into the semi-solid food is rather slow.

Nutritive value. Hommos b'tehineh is considered to be a nutritious food, because its principal ingredient is a legume, supplemented with sesame meal and a vegetable oil. It is rich in proteins and calories and was found to have the following composition for 100 g of edible portion:
- Energy value *(kcal)* 300
- Moisture 49.5
- Protein 9.6
- Lipids 19.7
- Carbohydrates 17.8

Lentils

Lentils (*Lens esculenta*) come second to fava beans in consumption as a traditional food in Egypt. Lentils are also consumed in other countries of the Near East, generally in three forms: soup, paste and koshary (a mixture of lentils with rice). All three types are usually prepared and consumed at household level, shops serving food and restaurants (for koshary see p. 32).

Preparation. Lentil soup is prepared by cooking sorted, washed and decorticated lentils in about three times their weight in water and boiling the mixture until the lentils acquire a desirable soft texture. The lentils are then homogenized and passed through a special sieve with an aperture of about 2 mm to separate the fibres and foreign matters. Small stones, if any, are separated by gravity by allowing the lentil-water blend to be decanted slowly, leaving the heavy impurities to sink to the bottom of the container. The blend is then reboiled for a few additional minutes for complete cooking. Water may be added to obtain the desirable consistency for soup, or excess water may be evaporated to obtain a paste consistency. Salt, spices and/or garlic and onions are usually added. Some rice may also be added to

TABLE 29
Proximate gross composition of lentils
(value per 100 g edible portion)

Component	Value
Energy value *(kcal)*	385
Protein *(g)*	25
Lipids *(crude ether extract) (g)*	0.9
Ash *(g)*	2
Crude fibre *(g)*	2
Carbohydrates *(g)*	70

the paste to let it acquire a desirable thick consistency. Traditionally, fried, cut onions are used to decorate the surface of the paste after it is poured in dishes and cooled. Very often oil is also added to the soup just before eating, and butter or ghee is added to the paste during cooking.

Lentil soup is also canned. After cooking, the soup is packed in cans and exhausted for 15 minutes at 96°C. The cans are then double-seamed and sterilized for about 15 minutes at a pressure of two atmospheres, depending on the size of cans.

Quick-cooking or instant lentil soup is made by boiling decorticated cracked lentils in about three times their weight in water for about 25 minutes, then dehydrating the product on plates in a drying cabinet, initially at 200°C for three minutes, then at 100°C for about six hours. The product is then packed in polyethylene bags and sealed. For domestic consumption, the dehydrated product is rehydrated and cooked in an equal weight of water for six minutes.

Nutritive value. Lentil food, sometimes referred to as lentil soup, usually contains 60 percent moisture and is quite high in protein (see Table 29). However, like other legume proteins, it is limiting in sulphur-containing amino-acids and should be supplemented with other foods rich in methionine whenever possible. Cooked lentils are considered to be rich in phosphorus and potassium and low in available iron.

Lupine seeds

Lupine seeds (*Lupinus termis*) are rich in protein and are consumed as a traditional food in Egypt, the Sudan and most of the countries of the Near East. This food is usually consumed after debittering as a snack at any time of day, especially among school children. It is extensively consumed during spring, and especially on national Spring Day, referred to in Egypt as *shamm el-nesiem*, which is concurrent with Easter Day.

Preparation. Lupine seeds are prepared for human consumption by various methods, all aiming at the removal of the alkaloids that account for the seeds' bitter taste. The first step of the debittering process is cleaning and sorting the seeds to remove chaff, pieces of dry clay and other foreign matters. They are then presteeped in about five times their weight in water for about five hours. This process may be repeated several times using fresh water each time. At the end of this process, the seeds increase in volume and acquire a soft texture. They are then boiled for about 30 minutes in fresh water, after which they are washed and soaked in running water for at least two days (or soaked in water for a few days with occasional changing of the soaking water) to remove the alkaloids causing the bitter taste. This debittering process removes the alkaloids almost completely. The seeds at this stage would have an agreeable taste free from bitterness; they are sold on the retail market after being wrapped in small paper bags.

Nutritive value. Lupine seeds are among the members of the leguminosae, which are high in their content of crude fibre and fat, but low in carbohydrate and moderate in protein. They also have a high calcium content but a low phosphorus content. Sulphur-containing amino-acids and tryptophan are the first and second limiting amino-acids respectively. Debittering causes threonine, proline and phenylalanine to increase, whereas glutamic acid, glycine, isoleuocine and tyrosine remain unchanged, and all other amino-acids exhibit considerable reduction. For the composition of lupine seeds, see Table 30.

TABLE 30
Proximate gross composition of raw and debittered lupine seeds
(value per 100 g, dry-weight basis)

Component	Raw seeds	Debittered seeds
Energy value *(kcal)*	403.3	425.3
Moisture *(g)*	10.2	20.5
Crude protein *(g)*	38.3	39.9
Crude lipids *(g)*	11.5	13.5
Carbohydrates *(g)*	32.5	30
Alkaloids *(g)*	1.5	0.01
Ash *(g)*	3.4	1.7

Fenugreek seeds

Fenugreek seeds (*Trigonella foenum-graecum* L.) belong to the legume family and are cultivated and used as a food in various forms in Egypt, the Sudan and other countries of the Near East, especially the Arab countries.

Fenugreek seeds are used to brew a popular hot beverage, especially in winter, and the boiled seeds are eaten with honey or syrups. They are also sprouted and eaten as a popular snack food. The leafy part of the green plant has a characteristic, pleasant taste and is very popular among children. Flour prepared from fenugreek seeds is also used, among other ingredients, for the preparation of spices and curry powder. The flour is added as a filling material in the production of some local sausages and as a supplement to wheat and corn (maize) flours used for baking certain types of bread in rural areas.

Preparation. The first step in preparation of sprouted fenugreek seeds is sorting and cleaning a certain quantity of seeds to remove chaff, stones and other foreign matters; the seeds are then washed with water and soaked for

TABLE 31
Proximate gross composition and nutritive value of dry and germinated fenugreek seeds (value per 100 g, dry-weight basis)

Component	Dry seeds	Germinated seeds *
Energy value *(kcal)*	400	378
Moisture *(g)*	11.1	66.1
Crude protein *(g)*	33.8	35.1
Lipids *(g)*	7.5	4.7
Soluble sugars *(g)*	8.7	6.4
Carbohydrates (other than soluble sugars) *(g)*	40.6	42.5
Crude fibre *(g)*	5.8	8.3
Ash *(g)*	3.5	3
Sodium *(mg)*	130	218
Potassium *(mg)*	32.3	18.9
Calcium *(mg)*	186	158
Magnesium *(mg)*	152	140
Phosphorus *(mg)*	348	402
Zinc *(mg)*	4.1	5
Copper *(mg)*	2.9	2.2
Iron *(mg)*	21.6	17.8

* Three days

24 hours in about five times their weight in water. The wet seeds are covered with a damp cloth and left for 12 more hours in the dark to germinate. On a commercial scale, the washed seeds are germinated in special earthenware cones fitted with a hole of about 1 cm in diameter at the narrow end of the cone. Radicles grow and occupy the whole volume of the cone. They are usually displayed for sale as such.

Nutritive value. Upon germination, the moisture content of fenugreek seeds increases considerably, and the lipids and soluble sugars moderately decrease. Table 31 illustrates its composition.

Glutamic and asparatic acids are the most abundant amino-acids in fenugreek seeds, followed by leucine, arginine, lysine and proline. After germination, the levels of asparatic acid, phenylalanine, tyrosine, threonine, tryptophan and valine increase, while those of glutamic-acid proline decrease.

The importance of fenugreek seeds in nutrition lies in the fact that they have a high lysine and tryptophan content, whereas cysteine and methionine are only present to a low extent. Therefore, fenugreek can provide the essential amino-acids that are known to be deficient in cereals. Fenugreek-seed flour is a good supplement of essential amino-acids when added to wheat flour in baking some types of traditional bread. When the seeds are eaten alone, they supplement the diet with essential amino-acids.

Bibliography

Abdel Aal, E.M. 1983. *Chemical and technological studies on some legumes and rice as source of protein*. Dept Food Science and Technology, Faculty of Agriculture, Univ. Alexandria. (M.Sc. thesis)

Abdel Aal, M.H. 1986. Changes in gross composition with emphasis on lipid and protein fractions during germination of fenugreek seeds. *Food Chem.*, 22: 193.

Abdel Kader, M.M., Adham, K., Eissa, M., Abdel, M. & Hodhod, S. 1975. Nutritive value of lentils. *Bull. Nutrition Inst., Cairo, Egypt*, 5(1): 99.

Abdel Naby, A. 1980. *Studies on Egyptian rice*. Dept Food Science and Technology, Faculty of Agriculture, Univ. Alexandria. (M.Sc. thesis)

Abdou, I.A. & Fikri, I.E. 1967. Protein-rich food mixtures of cereals and legumes. *Bull. Nutrition Inst., Cairo, Egypt*, 3(1): 1978.

Abu Salah, M.S.A. 1970. *Chemical and technological studies on burghol in the UAR*. Dept Food Science and Technology, Faculty of Agriculture, Univ. Alexandria. (M.Sc. thesis)

Abu Samaha, R.O. 1983. *Chemical, technological and nutritional studies on lentils*. Dept Food Science and Technology, Faculty of Agriculture, Univ. Alexandria. (M.Sc. thesis)

Alani, M. 1987. *Etude de la valeur nutritive des préparations culinaires marocaines à base de céréales*. Mémoire de fin d'études, Institut agronomique et vétérinaire Hassan II, Rabat.

Al Zayani, A.R. 1988. *A taste of the Arabian Gulf*, p. 11. Bahrain, Government Press.

Amin, K.A. 1979. *A study of the relative nutritive value of some plant proteins in Egypt*. Dept Nutrition, High Institute of Public Health, Univ. Alexandria. (M.Sc. thesis)

Burnet, E. & Viscontini M. 1939. Le pain et les céréales dans l'alimentation tunisienne. *Arch. Inst. Pasteur, Tunis*, XXVIII: 221-268.

Dagher, S.M., Shadarevian, S. & Berbari, W. 1987. *J. Food. Sci.*, 52(6): 1600-1603.

Damir, A.A.H. 1978. *Chemical and technological studies on quality and staling of Egyptian bread*. Dept Food Science and Technology, Faculty of Agriculture, Univ. Alexandria. (Ph.D. thesis)

Desikachar, H.S.R. 1980. Development of weaning foods with high caloric density and low hot-paste viscosity using traditional technologies. *Food and Nutrition Bull.*, 2(4): 21-23.

El Gindy, M.M. 1964. The chemical analysis of cereals and cereal products. Cairo, *El Nahda Publ.* (in Arabic)

El Gindy, M.M., Abdou, I.A., Alian, A. & Mohamed, T.M. 1975. Effect of some preparation processes on the amino-acid content of lentils, kishk and fereek. *Bull. Nutrition Inst., Cairo, Egypt*, 5(1): 77.

El Mahdy, A.R. 1982. Effect of germination on the nitrogenous constituents, protein fractions, *in vitro* digestibility and antinutritional factors of fenugreek seeds *(Trigonella foenum graecum* L.*)*. *Food Chem.*, 8: 253.

El Mahdy, A.R. & El-Sebaiy, L.A. 1982. Changes in phytate and minerals during germination and cooking of fenugreek seeds. *Food Chem.*, 9: 149.

El Mahdy, A.R. & El Sebaiy, L.A. 1983. Changes in carbohydrates of germinating fenugreek seeds. *(Trigonella foenum graecum* L.*) J. Sci. Food Agric.*, 34: 951.

El Nahry, F.I., Murad, F.E., Khalil, S.M. & Bassily, N.S. 1980. Chemical composition and protein quality of lentils consumed in Egypt. *Qualitas Plantarum*, 30(2): 87.

El-Sebaiy, L.A. & El-Mahdy, A.R. 1983. Lipid changes during germination of fenugreek seeds *(Trigonella foenum graecum* L.*)*. *Food Chem.*, 10: 309.

El Shimi, N.M. 1975. *A study of some products of wheat flour*. Dept Food Science and Technology, Faculty of Agriculture, Univ. Alexandria. (M.Sc. thesis)

FAO. 1982. *Food composition tables for the Near East*. FAO Food and Nutrition Paper No. 26. Rome, Italy.

Gaafar, A.M. 1971. *Studies on precooked dehydrated soups*. Dept Food Science and Technology, Faculty of Agriculture, Univ. Alexandria. (M.Sc. thesis)

Gobert, E. 1940. Usages et rites alimentaires tunisiens. *Arch. Inst. Past. Tunis*, 29: 475-589.

Gobert, E. 1943. Les références historiques des nourritures tunisiennes. *Les Cahiers de Tunis*, III(12): 501-542.

Hamza, A.S. 1974. *Evaluation of protein quality of some Egyptian legumes*. Dept Food Science and Technology, Faculty of Agriculture, Univ. Cairo, Egypt. (Ph.D. thesis)

Hommeid, M.A. & Al Army, M.A. 1986. A study on the mechanization of fereekeh production in Jordan. *Dirassat*, 13(8): 73.

Hubert, A. 1984. *Le pain et l'olive: aspects de l'alimentation en Tunisie*. Centre régional de publication. Lyon, Editions du CNRS.

INS. 1975. *Table de composition des aliments tunisiens*. Institut national de la statistique. Claude Jardin, FAO Consultant, Tunis.

Kamar, Ayat E.A. 1977. *Chemical and technological studies on fenugreek powder*. Dept Food Science and Technology, Faculty of Agriculture, Univ. Alexandria. (M.Sc. thesis)

Kamel, B.S. & Allam, M. 1980. *Composition and protein quality of foods consumed in Kuwait (Phase II)*, p. 21. Kuwait Institute for Scientific Research.

Khalil, J.K., Sawaya, W.N., Safi, W.J. & Al-Mohammed, H.M. 1984. Chemical composition and nutritional quality of sorghum flour and bread. *Qual. Plant Foods Hum. Nutr.*, 34: 141-150.

Kouki, M. 1967. *La cuisine tunisienne "d'Ommok Sannafa"*. Tunis, SAEP.

Mesallam, A.S.F. 1976. *Chemical and technological studies on corn and wheat proteins*. Dept Food Science and Technology, Faculty of Agriculture, Univ. Alexandria. (Ph.D. thesis)

Mohamed, Abd Alla M. 1984. *Chemical and technological studies on lupine seeds (Lupinus termis) as a source of protein*. Dept Food Science and Technology, Faculty of Agriculture, Univ. Alexandria. (M.Sc. thesis)

Mohamed, A.M., Youssef, M.M., Aman, M.E. & Adel Shehata, A. 1987. Effect of debittering on chemical composition, functional properties and *in vitro* digestibility of lupine *(Lupinus termis)* flour. *J. Food Sci. (Egypt)*, 15(2): 161.

Moreau J. & Andry, R. 1942. Un aliment nord-africain: le couscous. *Arch. Inst. Past. Tunis*, 31: 302-310.

Musaiger, A.O., Al Mohizea, I.S., Al Kanhal, M.A. & Jaidah, J.H. 1989. Chemical and amino-acid composition of various breads consumed in Bahrain. *Ecol. Food Nutr.*, 21: 211-217.

Pellett, P.L. & Shadarevian, S. 1970. *Food composition tables for use in the Middle East*. Beirut, Lebanon, American University of Beirut Press.

Refaey, F.Y., Hamza, Y.A., Raya, A.W., Ahmed, S.A., Gholy, T.F., Bishay, R.G. & Madkour, Z.A. 1957. *Quality survey of Egyptian wheat crop (1956)*. Grain and Bread Res. La., Ministry of Agriculture, UAR.

Risk, S.S., Sedky, A. & Safwat Mohamed, M. 1960a. Studies on Egyptian bread: I. Types and methods of baking commercial bread in Egypt. II. Chemical composition of some types of bread consumed in various localities of Egypt. III. Changes in the main constituents of flour during fermentation and baking. *Alex. J. Agric. Res.*, 8(1): 83, 89, 99.

Sabry, Z.I. & Tannous, R.T. 1961. Effect of parboiling on the thiamine, riboflavin and niacin content of wheat. *Cereal Chem.*, 38: 536-539.

Sawaya, W.N., Khalil, J.K., Khatchadourian, H.A. & Al Mohammed, M.M. 1984. Nutritional evaluation of various breads consumed in Saudi Arabia. *Nutr. Rep. Int.*, 29: 1161-1170.

Shakieb, L. Abdel Hady. 1984. *Chemical and biological assessment of lentils and rice protein and their mixture ("Koshary")*. Dept Food Science and Technology, Faculty of Agriculture, Univ. Alexandria. (Ph.D. thesis)

Shakieb, L.A.E., Zoueil, M.E., Youssef, M.M. & Mohamed, M.S. 1985. Effect of cooking on the chemical composition of lentils, rice and their blend ("Koshary"). *Food Chem.*, 18: 163.

Shakieb, L.A.E., Zoueil, M.E., Youssef, M.M. & Mohamed, M.S. 1986. Fermentation and properties of instant lentils-rice blend ("Koshary"). *Alex. J. Agric. Res.*, 31(3): 207.

Shakieb, L.A.E., Zoueil, M.E., Youssef, M.M. & Mohamed, M.S. 1986. Amino acid composition and *in vitro* digestibility of lentils and rice proteins and their mixtures ("Koshary"). *Food Chem.*, 20: 61.

Shakieb, L.A.E., Youssef, M.M., Zoueil, M.E. & Mohamed, M.S. 1987. Protein quality of lentils, rice and their blend ("Koshary"), as affected by cooking. *Alex. J. Agric. Res.*, 32(1): 193.

Yaker, L. (née Rahmani). 1976. *Rites et pratiques alimentaires à Aokas* (Wilaya de Bejaia-Algérie). (Thèse de doctorat d'Etat) Université René Descartes, Paris, France.

Younis, M.A.A. 1984. *Chemical and technological studies on utilization of new maize variety flours in Egyptian bread.* Dept Food Science and Technology, Faculty of Agriculture, Univ. Alexandria. (Ph.D. thesis)

Youssef, M.M. 1978. *A study of factors affecting cookability of faba beans (Vicia faba L.).* Dept Food Science and Technology. Faculty of Agriculture, Univ. Alexandria. (Ph.D. thesis)

Youssef, M.M., Hamza, M.A., Abdel Aola, M.H., Shakieb, L.A. & El Banna, A.A. 1986. Amino acid composition and *in vitro* digestibility of some Egyptian foods made from faba beans *(Vicia faba* L.). *Food Chem.*, 22: 225.

Youssef, M.M., Abdel Aola, M.H., Hamza, M.A. & El Banna, A.A. 1987. Chemical composition of some Egyptian foods made from faba beans *(Vicia faba* L.). *Die Nahrung*, 31(2): 185.

Youssef, M.M., Abdel Aola, M.H., Shakieb, L.A. & Ziena, H.N. 1987. Effect of dehulling, soaking and germination on chemical composition, mineral elements and protein patterns of faba beans *(Vicia faba* L.). *Food Chem.*, 23: 129.

Youssef, M.M., Mesallam, S.A., El Shimi, M.A. & El Banna, A.A. 1988. Some chemical constituents of Egyptian faba beans *(Vicia faba* L.). *J. Coll. Agric., King Saud Univ.*, 10(1): 59.

Chapter 2
Milk and milk products

FRESH MILK
Camel milk

The camel was and is still the vehicle of transport for the Bedouin community in the Arab Gulf states and in some other parts of the Arab world. It plays an important role in supplying the desert dwellers with milk as well as meat, especially under the unfavourable conditions prevailing in the desert.

Camel milk *(haleeb al-jamal)* is usually drunk fresh as raw milk by desert dwellers. This practice can be hazardous to their health. In Saudi Arabia, however, camel milk was recently produced commercially as a pasteurized milk. This milk is considered a favourite food by Bedouins, even by those who have shifted to urban areas.

Since camel milk is the main source of protein and minerals for some desert dwellers, more attention should be paid to camel breeding and selection in order to increase the quantity and to improve the quality of the milk produced. This attention is particularly important when we consider that camels have a better potential to adapt very well to the harsh environment of the desert than goats and cows do.

Table 32 illustrates the composition and mineral content of camel milk.

FERMENTED MILKS
Zabady

Zabady or *laban* is a traditional type of yoghurt. It is usually made from buffalo milk in Egypt, but milk from cows, sheep or goats is also used.

Preparation. Zabady is usually prepared at home in both rural and urban areas; it is also manufactured on a commercial scale. At home, milk is boiled for a few minutes and then left to cool to 37°C-45°C. A starter is then added

TABLE 32
Proximate gross composition and mineral content of camel milk
(value per 100 g edible portion)

Component	Value
Energy value *(kcal)*	101
Moisture *(g)*	87.5
Protein *(g)*	2.7
Lipids *(g)*	3.3
Carbohydrates *(g)*	5.3
Ash *(g)*	0.8
Calcium *(mg)*	114.8
Phosphorus *(mg)*	83.8
Iron *(mg)*	0.2
Sodium *(mg)*	58.8
Zinc *(mg)*	0.4

to the milk and mixed thoroughly. The inoculated milk is then distributed into earthenware pots or other containers. They are then incubated for a few hours. In Egypt or the Sudan, milk is sometimes incubated in wooden boxes heated by charcoal where the temperature is controlled manually. When the milk begins to coagulate, the source of heat is removed, and the pots are left until the milk sets. The pots are then transferred to a cool place or a refrigerator to slow down the development of lactic acid, since excess acid develops an objectionable sour taste and may cause the separation of whey.

On a commercial scale, zabady is prepared in large plants following the same basic steps. Modern equipment is utilized, especially automatically controlled incubators. Usually the product is packed in plastic containers fitted with loose plastic caps and kept cool until consumed.

Nutritive value. Due to variations in the chemical composition of milk and the differences in heat treatments or types of starters used, the chemical

TABLE 33
Proximate gross composition and mineral and vitamin content of zabady (value per 100 g, wet-weight basis)

Component	Value
Energy value *(kcal)*	61
Moisture *(g)*	86.4
Protein *(g)*	4.9
Lipids *(g)*	2.8
Lactose *(g)*	4.6
Ash *(g)*	0.8
Phosphorus *(mg)*	107.2
Calcium *(mg)*	138.2
Iron *(mg)*	0.06
Zinc *(mg)*	0.38
Magnesium *(mg)*	12.6
Thiamine *(µg)*	51.3
Riboflavin *(µg)*	180
Cyanocobalamine *(µg)*	0.07

composition and quality of different zabady samples differ considerably. For a proximate analysis, see Table 33.

Laban or rayeb

Laban is the name given to yoghurt in the Gulf region; it is also known as *rayeb* in the Maghreb countries. Laban is traditionally prepared from cow, sheep or goat milk. It has a slightly acid taste and a pleasant aroma resembling that of buttermilk.

Preparation. Fresh milk is poured into a pot and covered with a piece of cloth. The milk is left for natural fermentation at ambient temperature overnight. Old laban is added sometimes as a starter. If the ambient

TABLE 34
Proximate gross composition and mineral content of *laban*
(value per 100 g edible portion)

Component	Value
Energy value *(kcal)*	50
Moisture *(g)*	90.5
Protein *(g)*	3.6
Lipids *(crude ether extract) (g)*	3.2
Ash *(g)*	0.7
Lactose *(g)*	2
Calcium *(mg)*	121
Phosphorus *(mg)*	95
Sodium *(mg)*	130

temperature is too low, i.e. during winter, the milk is placed in a warm place to speed up the fermentation process. When the curd is formed, cream is separated by skimming or by churning in a goat's skin for one or two hours, after which it is ready for consumption.

The following bacteria were isolated from this milk: *Streptococcus lactis, Streptococcus kefir, Lactobacillus casei,* and coliforms (as contaminants).

Nowadays, laban is prepared in large dairy plants from cow's whole milk, and the yoghurt starter has replaced natural fermentation.

Nutritive value. The composition of laban varies according to the type of milk used. Chemical composition of laban made of cow's milk is shown in Table 34.

Lben
Lben or *zebda arbi* is the name given in the Maghreb countries to the same food known as *shaneenah* or *makheed* in Jordan. A sour milk or buttermilk, it is considered a secondary product of fermented milk churning. It has a sour

taste and thick consistency, containing suspended particles of milk curd and unremoved butter. This dairy product is often consumed as a drink with meals, specially during spring and summer. In Jordan, it is used in the production of *gemead* (see p. 59).

Preparation. The first step in producing lben is the fermentation of milk to obtain rayeb or yoghurt. The fermented milk is then put in a *shekwa* or *kerbah*, which is a bag used for churning. This bag is the skin of a sheep or goat, removed undamaged so that it forms a tight container when the openings are tied. The neck opening acts as the mouth of the vessel.

Churning is usually carried out in the morning. For this purpose, the shekwa is filled with rayeb and expanded with air. Then it is closed tightly and shaken vigorously for about half an hour, until the fat globules coalesce. The formation of butter is judged by a change in the sound produced during shaking. Butter is then removed by hand. To help the formation of butter, water is usually added, warm or cold depending on the season. The remaining milk after the removal of butter is called makheed or lben. This product as expected has a mixed microbial flora composed mainly of lactic-acid bacteria, enterobacteria and yeasts. Its nutritional value is shown in Table 35.

The acidity of lben results from the fermentation of lactose into lactic acid during the coagulation phase. This spontaneous fermentation may result in a high acidity level exceeding 11 to 14 g of lactic acid per litre, which gives the product a markedly sour taste. Because this fermentation is uncontrolled, other types of fermenting agents may also be involved. Alcoholic or pepotonic fermentation occurring at the same time may give a strong taste and smell to lben that affect its acceptability.

Lben is being produced and marketed on a large scale in Tunisia and other Maghreb countries. It is a nutritious food that has good keeping qualities. At the family level, preparation of lben is a long process comporting serious risks of contamination. To facilitate the preparation of lben, coagulation should be speeded up by adding a fermentation agent. Clean containers and proper handling of milk during milking and fermentation are very important for the physical and biological qualities of the final product. It is particularly

TABLE 35
Proximate gross composition of Iben
(value per 100 g edible portion)

Component	Value
Energy value *(kcal)*	64
Moisture *(g)*	88.5
Protein *(g)*	3.5
Lipids *(crude ether extract) (g)*	3.4
Carbohydrates *(g)*	4.1

important that the shekwa be washed after each churning operation and its outer surface sprinkled with salt to prevent the formation of mucilaginous substances. In this way, the taste and consistency of lben is enhanced (less sour, thicker) and its keeping quality improved.

Since this product is prepared from unpasteurized milk, it could constitute a health hazard, as it might transmit some pathogenic micro-organisms to man like *Brucella*, which causes Malta fever.

Labneh

Labneh is a typical Near Eastern food that is very easily prepared from yoghurt. It is a very popular breakfast food that can be eaten as a spread on sandwiches or rolled into balls and stored in oil in glass jars.

Preparation. Labneh is yoghurt that has been strained to separate its whey component, usually by straining the yoghurt through cloth bags for several hours. This concentration process allows further fermentation by the lactic-acid bacteria, resulting in a modified flavour of the final product.

Yoghurt is prepared by inoculating pasteurized milk with *Lactobacillus bulgaricus* and *Streptococcus thermopholis* in the form of a starter culture. Incubation is carried out at 42°C-45°C for five hours. Improvement in the quality of labneh can be obtained if the whey is separated from the yoghurt

TABLE 36
Proximate gross composition of *labneh*
(value per 100 g edible portion)

Component	Value
Energy value *(kcal)*	154
Moisture *(g)*	74
Protein *(g)*	13
Lipids *(crude ether extract) (g)*	10
Ash *(g)*	1.6
Carbohydrates *(g)*	1

by low-speed centrifugation. Furthermore, to improve the shelf-life of labneh, yoghurt can be pasteurized before centrifugation, but care must be taken not to destroy the structure of the curd.

Nutritive value. Labneh is an excellent food, since it is usually consumed with bread, oil and some fresh vegetables. It serves as a concentrated source of protein (see Table 36).

Gemead
Gemead is a defatted, dehydrated yoghurt that is usually prepared in spring or summer. It is believed to be of Turkish origin and is widely consumed in Jordan, the Syrian Arab Republic and parts of Iraq and Saudi Arabia.

Preparation. The starting material is sheep or goat milk. Cow milk is rarely used. The first step is to prepare fermented milk or to convert the milk to yoghurt by inoculating it with lactic-acid bacteria and incubating it at 42°C for several hours. The butterfat of the yoghurt is separated by churning. This process causes the fat globules to agglomerate and float. Traditionally, the churning is performed by prolonged shaking in a bag made of goat skin usually called a *shekwa*. The butterfat adheres to the skin and is separated and used for the preparation of *samneh*. Removal of the fat at this stage prevents any development of rancidity later on during dehydration. The defatted yoghurt, called shaneenah or makheed, is concentrated by straining the whey through a cloth using high pressure. The residue is then salted to the level of 3 percent and shaped by hand in the form of small balls. The balls are placed in the sun and rotated occasionally until dry. The product is usually stored in a dark, well aerated place for long periods of time without need of refrigeration.

Nutritive value. Gemead is a concentrated yoghurt that is usually reconstituted to a thick consistency before consumption. Thus, it represents a rich source of excellent-quality protein. It is eaten with such traditional foods as mansaf and kabseh. It was found to contain 50 percent protein and 20 percent fat.

Kishk

Kishk is a popular food commonly prepared and used in many countries of the Near East, especially the Arab countries. It is a fermented and dried food mixture eaten usually at breakfast, lunch or dinner. It is mainly prepared by rurals as a home industry to be marketed in urban areas. The food keeps for a long time without refrigeration and has excellent nutritive value.

Preparation. The ingredients used in the preparation of kishk are yoghurt or naturally fermented milk (cow, sheep or goat) and burghol or wheat flour. Two parts of fermented milk and one part of burghol are mixed thoroughly with the addition of about 3 percent (w/w) of salt, and the mixture is left for 24 hours in a warm place to ferment. The fermented mixture acquires a pasty consistency. It is then formed into balls and left to ferment and dry in the sun on straw mats for about seven days. The dried balls are then ground into fine granules. The resulting product, named kishk, is packed in sacks of cloth or packaged and sold in retail shops. Since this food is not hygroscopic, it can be stored in open containers for a long time without deterioration.

This food has a good shelf-life, because it is high in acid and is quite dry. Contamination during sundrying and development of rancidity are the

TABLE 37
Proximate gross composition of *kishk*
(value per 100 g edible portion)

Component	Value
Energy value *(kcal)*	391
Moisture *(g)*	13
Protein *(g)*	15.9
Lipids *(crude ether extract) (g)*	11.9
Ash *(g)*	5.6
Crude fibre (g)	1.8
Nitrogen re-extract (g)	51.8

major problems faced by the processor. It is expected that the quality of the food can be greatly improved if dehydration is carried out under controlled conditions, such as drum drying, and the final product kept as flakes or ground to a powder. The colour and flavour of the food can be greatly improved by this process and its production period may be extended to the entire year instead of being limited to the summer season.

Nutritive value. Because kishk is a combination of milk and wheat, the supplementary effects that these components have on each other, particularly in terms of the amino-acid balance, make kishk an extremely desirable food from the point of view of its nutritional value (see Table 37). It is high in calories and is considered a good source of calcium and phosphorus. It is easily digested and is particularly rich in the sulphur-containing amino-acid, cysteine.

Uggot or madeer

Uggot or *madeer* is a dried, fermented-milk product with buttermilk flavour that is made from goat or sheep milk. It is made in different shapes and is cream or pale yellow in colour. Known in Saudi Arabia, it is commonly consumed by desert dwellers, and plays an important role in providing them with essential nutrients. It is usually prepared when there is a surplus of milk production; when there is a shortage of milk supply, however, uggot is dissolved in water and drunk or eaten with dates.

Preparation. Uggot is prepared by allowing the milk to undergo natural fermentation overnight. The fermented milk is then manually churned in a home-made churner (made from sheep or goat skin) for one half to two hours to facilitate the separation of fat. The remaining buttermilk is boiled until most of the water is evaporated. The dough-like paste is then allowed to cool to ambient temperature. The paste is then shaped by hand into small pieces (50 g each). The pieces are covered by a cloth and allowed to dry under direct sunlight for two to four days.

Nutritive value. The low moisture content as well as the low pH of uggot allow the product to be stored for a long time (about one year) at room temperature without any detrimental changes. Uggot is a rich source of protein. The essential amino-acids in uggot were found to be higher than the FAO/WHO reference protein (see Table 38).

CHEESES
Domiati cheese
White cheese *(gibneh beydah)* in many Arab countries, or *domiati* cheese (after the city and governorate of Damietta located in the northeast section of the Egyptian delta), is a soft cheese. It is believed to have originated in Egypt around 332 BC. It is also made and consumed throughout the Arab world. It may be made from cow, buffalo, goat or sheep milk. It is a very popular cheese and when fresh, it possesses a soft body of distinctive flavour and rather salty taste. As it ripens in brine, it acquires a firmer texture and an acidic taste. As ripening proceeds, the texture becomes closed with no holes, then becomes slightly flaky and brittle. An appetizing flavour develops gradually during pickling, accompanied by a change in colour to light amber.

TABLE 38
Proximate gross composition and mineral content of *uggot*
(value per 100 g edible portion)

Component	Value
Energy value *(kcal)*	427
Moisture *(g)*	3.9
Protein *(g)*	35.5
Lipids *(crude ether extract) (g)*	15.3
Ash *(g)*	7.9
Crude fibre *(g)*	0.5
Carbohydrates *(g)*	36.9
Calcium *(mg)*	982
Phosphorus *(mg)*	957
Iron *(mg)*	2.5
Sodium *(mg)*	477
Zinc *(mg)*	1.4

Preparation. The starting material is buffalo or cow milk (or a mixture of both in Egypt), and sheep and/or goat milk in many other countries. The manufacturing process in different dairies varies only with respect to the size of batches. The process is characterized by salting the milk at the very first step of manufacture to counteract any bacteriological defects in the raw milk and, among other objectives, to avoid the formation of gas holes and abnormal flavour in the end product. The salt concentration is variable and depends upon the atmospheric temperature of the season, the previous treatment of milk and the intended storage period.

The manufacturing process starts by heating one-third of the standardized milk (8 percent, 4 percent and 2 percent fat, for full-cream, half-cream and quarter-cream cheese respectively) to 80°C in jacketed metal containers. Salt is added to the other two-thirds of the batch at a concentration ranging between 5-14 percent. For cheese intended to be stored in refrigerators, the concentration of added salt ranges between 5-6 percent in winter, 6-7 percent in spring and autumn and 7-8 percent in summer. For cheese intended to be stored at ambient temperature, the concentration of added salt ranges between 8-14 percent. The two portions of hot and salted cold milk are then mixed together, and the temperature of the resulting mixture drops to about 35-40°C. The milk is held at this temperature, and preferably at 38°C, by passing hot water in the jackets. Heating this way helps to decrease the number of micro-organisms in the milk while improving the consistency of the end product. Milk is then renneted by the addition of 10-15 ml of standard liquid calf rennet to each 45.5 kg (100 lb) of milk. Rennet substitutes from animal, plant or microbial sources have been investigated and used; porcine products, however, are not used in Egypt and the Sudan nor in any of the Arab or Islamic countries.

After coagulation of the milk, which usually takes place within two to three hours, the coagulum is ladled out into moulds of wood or metal, which are lined with a coarse cloth or netting. Small-sized moulds are used by small dairies, while large ones are used for industrial-scale manufacture. In the former, moulds are turned frequently to drain the whey (usually two times per day for three days), while in the latter, the curd is put under gradually increasing pressure for about four days. Drainage time ranges between 12-24 hours. For fresh consumption, the moulds are removed prior to marketing, and the cheese is then cut into square pieces (about 8 cm per side and 3.5 cm in thickness) and wrapped in waxed paper.

Batches of cheese destined for storage are pickled by holding in salted whey for four to eight months. The cheese is cut into rectangular pieces or into cylindrical shapes of different dimensions, packed in suitable tins and completely covered with brine.

Some dairies apply certain modifications in the classical procedure for domiati-cheese processing, such as pasteurization and homogenization of the milk to avoid excessive salting and to retain the characteristic flavour and improve the cheese texture. In such cases a starter is added to the milk prior to manufacture.

The traditional method of preparing this cheese in Saudi Arabia and the Gulf countries is different and relies on a crude mixture of enzymes

TABLE 39
Proximate gross composition of *domiati* cheese
(value per 100 g edible portion)

Component	Value
Energy value *(kcal)*	511
Moisture *(g)*	55
Protein *(g)*	21.1
Lipids *(crude ether extract)* *(g)*	23.4
Ash *(g)*	2.6

produced in the stomach of suckling lambs. After birth, the lamb is nursed for one day and then killed. The coagulated milk (natural curd) is then removed from the lamb's stomach, wrapped tightly in a cloth and sundried for three to four days. The cloth containing the coagulated milk is then immersed three to four times in raw milk. When the milk coagulates, it is vigorously mixed by hand until the curd is broken into small pieces. These pieces are then properly packaged in brine and become ready for consumption. Table 39 illustrates the nutritive value of domiati cheese.

Kariesh cheese
Kariesh cheese is actually a defatted, soft, white cheese. It is one of the most popular, fresh lactic cheeses usually consumed at breakfast in both rural and urban areas in Egypt and the Sudan and most of the Arab countries. It is made of defatted buffalo or cow milk or a mixture of both. Although total annual production of kariesh cheese in Egypt and the Sudan is not known, it is believed that almost 50 percent of the total milk production is utilized in making this type of cheese.

Preparation. According to the traditional method, the buffalo or cow is milked directly into special earthenware jars known as *shalia* or *zeer* with a capacity of about 4-7 kg. The milk jars are kept undisturbed in a suitable place so that the fat may rise and form a surface layer, leaving the defatted milk underneath, which may sour or clot. This gravity-defatting process is usually completed within 24-36 hours during summer and two to three days during winter. After skimming the cream layer, the curd is poured into a reed-type (*Juncus* sp.) mat to drain. After a few hours, the mat ends are tied together to squeeze the curd and permit additional draining of whey. The mat is unfolded again and the curd is spread thereover as before. This process of squeezing and spreading of the curd is repeated once or twice, and finally the mat is hung from its joint ends, with its contents suspended, to help complete the drainage of whey, a process that usually takes two to three days. The cheese is then cut into suitable pieces and salted to taste using dry salt. It is then left a few more hours in the mat until no more whey drains off. The cheese is then ready for consumption.

On large commercial-scale manufacture, kariesh cheese is prepared in big dairy plants using mechanically standardized skimmed milk as a starting material and following a procedure similar to domiati-cheese manufacture. However, skimmed milk is not salted as is the case with the traditional processing method, and curdling is initiated by a starter. Dairy plants may also pasteurize and homogenize the skimmed milk before curdling in order to improve the flavour and texture of the final product. Coagulation of milk may also be accomplished enzymatically by rennet rather than by a starter to give better flavour and superior quality. Very little amount of rennet may also be added to the milk after addition of the starter to reduce the coagulation period to 16-18 hours.

Nutritive value. The quality and composition of kariesh cheese may vary considerably because of a number of factors such as quality and composition of the clotted skim milk, method of manufacture, time required to complete the drainage of whey, quality of added salt and method of handling the finished product. However, kariesh cheese contains many of the skim-milk constituents including protein, lactose, some of the water soluble vitamins and most of the calcium and phosphorus compounds originally present in milk (see Table 40).

TABLE 40
Proximate gross composition and nutritive value of *kariesh* cheese
(value per 100 g, wet-weight basis)

Component	Value
Energy value *(kcal)*	122
Moisture *(g)*	69
Protein *(g)*	17
Lipids *(g)*	6
Ash *(g)*	6
Sodium chloride *(mg)*	4.5
pH value *(mg)*	4.3
Titratable acidity *(mg)*	1.8

Mish

Mish is a traditional soft, pickled, ripened cheese. It has been known to the Egyptians since early times, as evidenced by drawings in ancient tombs. The product is characterized by a yellowish-brown colour, sharp flavour and high salt content. It is a common custom among housewives, especially in rural areas, to prepare their own mish at any time during the year, but since milk is abundant in winter, more mish is prepared during this season. Mish is usually made from kariesh cheese and less frequently from whole-milk domiati cheese; sometimes portions of other hard cheeses are added to the mish mixture to increase the fat content of the product.

Preparation. Details of making mish differ from region to region and from home to home in the same region; the basic steps in the procedure, however, are essentially the same. It starts by preparing kariesh cheese, which is then divided into cubes of about 8 cm each side and then packed under microaerophylic conditions in a large and clean earthenware pot known as a *ballas*. Spaces between the pieces of cheese are filled with either whole milk, skimmed milk or buttermilk (laban khad) containing 10 percent salt.

Old mish, in a proportion of about 2-7 percent of the whole mixture is added as a natural starter. Furthermore, a group or all of the following additives are usually added to the mixture to give the finished product its characteristic flavour and texture. These are:
- sesame seed *kosba* (the cake remaining after extraction of oil from sesame seeds);
- *morta*, the residue formed by boiling butter for the manufacture of butter oil (known as *samna*);
- spices such as:
  fenugreek *seed flour (Trigonella foenum-graecum* L.)
  red pepper *(Capsicum frutescens* var. *fasciculatum)*
  hot pepper *(cf. var. chilli)*
  paprika *(cf. var. tetragonium)*
  black pepper *(Piper nigrum);*
- Grains and/or flours of:
  anise seeds *(Pimpinella anisum)*
  common caraway *(Carlina caraui)*
  cumin *(Cuminum cyminum)*
  fennel *(Foeniculum officinale)*
  pick tooth *(Ammi visnaga)*
  cloves *(Eugenia caryophyllata* Thumb)
  nutmeg *(Myristica fragrans* Houttyn*)*
  thyme *(Thymus vulgaris)*
  nigella *(Nigella sativa),* and
  sweet green pepper (cf. var. *grossum).*

A small cloth bag containing borax (sodium borate) is usually placed on the surface of the milk as a preservative and to inhibit *Pyophella casei* larvae which may contaminate the cheese during ripening. The ballas, which is usually filled to the neck by the milk-cheese mixture, is covered by palm-leaf-sheath fibres and a piece of cloth. It is then tightly sealed by means of a mud paste mixed with wheat chaff. The ballas is kept under this partially anaerobic condition for about one year in a warm sunny place to ripen, during which most pieces of cheese break and form a slurry.

TABLE 41
Proximate gross composition and nutritive value of *mish*
(value per 100 g, wet-weight basis)

Component	Value
Energy value *(kcal)*	149.5
Moisture *(g)*	60.1
Protein *(g)*	12.6
Lipids *(g)*	11
Ash *(g)*	11.9
Sodium chloride *(mg)*	11.5
Total solids *(g)*	39.8
pH value *(mg)*	5.6
Phosphorus *(mg)*	0.32
Calcium *(mg)*	0.36

Sometimes wooden barrels of about 80-100 kg capacity are used instead of a ballas. After ripening, the mish paste is thoroughly mixed, emptied into stainless steel vats and heated at 100°C for ten minutes. The resulting cheese is then packed in 0.5- or 1-kg plastic containers and stored under refrigeration until consumption.

Nutritive value. The chemical composition and nutritive value of mish differ greatly from one locality to another due to a lack of standardized materials, the type and amounts of additives employed and activity of the microflora involved. Evidently there are three types of fermentations involved in mish making: lactic-acid, proteolytic- and butyric-acid fermentations. Lactic-acid bacteria have little to do with flavour production but seem to be responsible for preparing the ground for other bacteria, the anaerobic spore formers of the butyric-acid group which are usually responsible for the characteristic flavour of mish. Its nutritive value is shown in Table 41.

Halloum cheese

Halloum is a semi-soft, brined cheese made from sheep milk, which is sometimes mixed with goat milk. It is mainly produced in the Republic of Cyprus, in Lebanon and to a minor extent in the Syrian Arab Republic.

Preparation. Fresh, raw sheep milk is usually used in the preparation of halloum cheese. The milk is warmed to 32-34°C, and rennin is added. Enough enzyme is used to cause coagulation in 40 minutes. The coagulum is then cut into small cubes of about 3 x 3 cm and stirred gently with the whey while heating to 40°C. After 20 minutes, the curd is collected and pressed at high pressure to remove the liquid whey. The resulting solid mass is then cut into blocks of about 15 x 10 x 3 cm. The albumin and other proteins are removed from the whey by heating to 90-95°C and the coagulated proteins collected and sold as a cheaper cheese called *areeshi*. The hot whey is then used to cook the halloum cheese blocks. The temperature of the whey is held at this level for 40-80 minutes. During this period, the cheese blocks float and are removed for salting and folding. The cheese is packaged in cans, in plastic packages or submerged in brined whey.

The heating step in halloum preparation improves the sanitary level of the final product. If mechanization of the process allows for aseptic handling and packaging, this kind of cheese may have a long shelf-life and should remain free of pathogenic organisms.

Nutritive value. Like many other cheeses, halloum is considered a concentrated food, rich in easily digested protein of high nutritive quality. It is also rich in fat, particularly when made of sheep's milk, and therefore is a concentrated source of energy.

Nabulsi cheese

Nabulsi cheese is one of the traditional, white, brined cheeses known in various countries of the Near East, particularly in Jordan and neighbouring countries. The name nabulsi means from Nablus, a town on the West Bank. It is usually produced from sheep or go milk.

Preparation. Sheep milk is heated to about 35°C and coagulated by rennet. The resulting curd is pressed in small portions (about 200 g) using a cheesecloth. The resulting cheese can be consumed as such, but it is usually boiled in brine (not less than 15 percent w/v) containing a mixture of two powdered spices: mastic gum *(Pistacia lentiscus)* and *mahaleb (Prunus mahaleb)* seeds. The boiling process, which requires five to 15 minutes, prolongs the shelf-life of the cheese and improves its texture and flavour.

Nutritive value. Nabulsi cheese is a concentrated food particularly rich in calories and proteins. It is reported to have the following composition per 100 g edible portion:
- Energy value *(kcal)*   288
- Moisture   44
- Protein   16
- Lipids   24
- Ash   16

Shankleesh

Shankleesh is a kind of ripened cheese that relies on wild moulds for flavour development. Usually it is prepared from sheep milk and is the only mouldy type of cheese produced in the Near East.

Preparation. Sheep milk is transformed into yoghurt, and the butterfat is separated, usually by vigorous shaking after the addition of some water to the yoghurt. The defatted laban or yoghurt is gently heated to coagulate the milk proteins, which form a precipitate called areeshi. The precipitate is collected by filtering through a cloth and then salted (2 percent) and peppered. The solid mass is then pressed by hand in the form of small balls and allowed to dry in the sun for a period of three days. The dried balls are then placed in large jars covered with a cloth (to keep the air circulating) and ripened for one month. During this time moulds grow and cover the surface of the cheese. The low moisture content does not allow bacteria to multiply; only moulds will grow and impart a special flavour to the cheese. The vegetative growth is then washed off, and the cheese balls covered completely

TABLE 42
Proximate gross composition of shankleesh
(value per 100 g edible portion, dry-weight basis)

Component	Value
Energy value *(kcal)*	215
Moisture *(g)*	44
Protein *(g)*	35
Lipids *(crude ether extract) (g)*	5.6
Ash *(g)*	12.2
Nitrogen re-extract *(g)*	51.8
Carbohydrates *(g)*	3

with ground thyme and allowed further dehydration before being stored in glass jars.

Nutritive value. Shankleesh is considered to be a very healthy food, since it is very rich in good-quality protein and relatively low in its fat content, unlike other cheeses of similar flavour (see Table 42).

Yemeni cheese

This hard cheese is typical of the southern province of Yemen. It is also produced in other parts of the country and is always smoked, using various plants for the source of smoke that impart to the cheese a typical brown colour and a characteristic flavour.

Preparation. Sheep and goat milk are commonly used for preparing Yemeni cheese after some cream of the milk is removed, following overnight storage. Cheese makers in Yemen rely on coagulating enzymes produced directly in the stomach of suckling lambs or calves. Usually the calf is killed when two to three weeks old. The stomach is removed and hung to dry, after which it is stored until needed. Prior to use, the dried stomach is dipped in water, then in milk and squeezed a few times to release some of its enzymes. It can be dried again and re-used later.

The treated milk is allowed to coagulate overnight, and the whey is removed by drainage through a basket made of date-palm leaves. At the end of the drainage period, which lasts for about 12 hours, the curd is pressed and shaped into flat and round discs of various thicknesses. It is then smoked for about 20 minutes using some herbs to generate the smoke. The smoking step darkens the colour of the cheese, hardens its surface and imparts to it a characteristic aroma. It also destroys surface micro-organisms, thus prolonging the shelf-life of the product.

The smoked cheese is sold unpacked in various sizes for immediate consumption.

BUTTER
Ghee

Ghee (also known as *samneh, samin, smen* and *dhan*) is a white or light yellow semi-soft food that has a distinctive butter-like flavour. Ghee is mainly produced for prolonged storage, because home-made butter deteriorates very quickly and cannot be stored at room temperature. Its processing technique is based on melting and dehydrating butter and then filtering it using cheese cloth. It is used for different purposes, such as frying, cooking and flavouring certain foods.

Preparation. The starting material for the preparation of ghee is fermented milk (yoghurt) produced through a natural microbial fermentation. Fresh milk may also be used in preparing ghee directly. The soured milk is churned in home-made churners, which separate butter from buttermilk. Butter may also be produced from cream, which is obtained by separating warm milk at 37°C using a cream separator. The collected butter is melted and heated to 110°C to bring the moisture content to the lowest level possible in the final product. Salt is sometimes added as a flavouring substance. Small quantities of wheat flour or semolina are used in this step to absorb the residual water content that may remain in the ghee.

TABLE 43
Proximate gross composition of *ghee*
(value per 100 g, wet-weight basis)

Component	Maghreb	Near East	Arabian Gulf
Energy value *(kcal)*	698	890	813
Moisture *(g)*	20	1	9.4
Protein *(g)*	0.9	-	0.3
Lipids *(g)*	77.3	99	90.2
Ash *(g)*	-	-	0.1
Carbohydrates *(g)*	1.5	-	-

The melted ghee is then filtered through a cheese cloth to remove the semolina particles and any precipitated protein. It is then poured into suitable containers and allowed to solidify for long-term storage.

Nutritive value. The energy value (kcal) provided by 100 g edible portion varies from 689 to 890 kcal in the Maghreb and Near East areas respectively, while it is 813 kcal in the Arabian Gulf. The reason for this variation is the moisture content left in the final product as shown in Table 43.

Bibliography

Abou-Donia, S.A. 1984. Egyptian fresh fermented milk products. *NZ J. Dairy Sci. and Tech.*, 19: 7.

Abou-Donia, S.A. 1986. Egyptian "Domiati" soft white pickled cheese. *NZ J. Dairy Sci. and Tech.*, 21: 167.

Abou-Donia, S.A. & El-Soda, M.A. 1986. Egyptian soft pickled ripened "Mish" cheese. *Indian J. Dairy Sci.*, 39: 1.

Abu-Lehia, I.H. 1987. Composition of camel milk. *Milchwissenschaft*, 42: 368-371.

Abu-Lehia, I.H. 1988. The chemical composition of jameed cheese. *Ecol. Food and Nutr.*, 29: 231-239.

Al-Mashhadi, A.S., Saadi, S.R., Ismail, A. & Salji, P. 1986. Traditional fermented dairy products in Saudi Arabia. *Cultured Dairy Product. J.*, 22: 24-26.

Basson, P., Abuirmeileh, N. 1980. *Food conservation in north-west Jordan*. FAO Report.

Dagher, S. & Ali, A. 1985. *J. Food Prot.*, 48(4): 399-302.

Dakroury, A.M., Aly, H.E. & Seddik, M.F. 1975. Effect of cooking on the nutritive value and microbiological quality of "Kishk" (Upper Egypt variety). *Bull. Nutr. Inst.*, UAR.

Davis, J.G. 1976. *Cheese. Manufacturing methods*, Edinburgh, UK. Churchill Livingstone.

El-Asphahani, A.M. 1972. *Nutritional evaluation of Egyptian national diets*. Dept Food Science and Technology, Faculty of Agriculture, Univ. Cairo.

El-Gindy, M.M. 1962. *The chemical analysis of cereals and cereal products*. Cairo, El-Nahda Publ. (in Arabic)

El-Rakshy, S. El-Din. 1968. *Microbiology of milk and milk products*. Dar el Maaref, Alexandria.

El-Sadek, G.M., Zawahry, M.R. & El-Mottaleb, A. 1958. Chemical composition of Egyptian "Kishk". *Indian J. Dairy Sci.*, 11: 67.

Hommeid, M.A. & Tukan, S. 1986. *Dirassat*, 13(5): 19-29.

Hommeid, M.A., Tikan, S.K. & Yamani, M.I. *Dirassat*, 14 (11): 179-186 (submitted for publication in *Milchwissenschaft*, 1989).

INS. 1975. *Table de composition des aliments tunisiens*. Institut national de la statistique. Claude Jardin, FAO Consultant, Tunis.

Kamel, B.S. & Allam, M. 1979. *Composition of foods consumed in Kuwait (Phase I)*, p. 15. Kuwait Institute for Scientific Research, Kuwait.

Mohamed, T.M. Abdel-Monem. 1971. *The effect of some preparation processes on the amino acid content of some local Egyptian foods*. Dept Food Science and Technology, Faculty of Agriculture, Univ. Alexandria. (M.Sc. thesis)

Pellett, P.L. & Shadarevian, S. 1970. *Food composition tables for use in the Middle East*. Beirut, Lebanon, American University of Beirut Press.

Sawaya, W.N., Kahn, P. & Al-Sahtat, A.F. 1984. Physical and chemical characteristics of ghee and butter from goat and sheep milk. *Food Chem.*, 14: 227-232.

Sawaya, W.M., Salji, J.P., Ayaz, M. & Khalil, J.K. 1984. The chemical composition and nutritive value of madeer. *Ecol. Food Nutr.*, 55: 29-37.

Steinkhaus, K.H. 1983. *Foods*. New York, Marcel Dekker.

Yamani, M.I. 1989. Personal communication.

Zaki, N. & Shokry, Y.M. 1988. Chemical and microbiological changes in "Mish" cheese and "Mish" during ripening. *Egyptian J. Dairy Sci.*, 16: 119.

Chapter 3
Meat, fish and their products

RAW MEAT
Camel meat
Although camel meat *(laham jamal)* is fresh meat, it is included in this volume since it is widely used in the region and typically specific to desert areas.

Camels are the principal animals that can tolerate the difficult environmental factors of the desert. Camels are raised for several purposes: for transport, for their milk and for their meat. Camel meat contains tough muscle fibres and has a characteristic flavour. The fat in the animal is mostly concentrated in the hump *(sanam)*. The camel breed living in the Arabian Gulf region has one hump, but other camel breeds in other Asian regions have two humps.

Camel meat is rarely available on the market. It is mostly consumed in the desert by the Bedouins, although many Bedouins living in urban areas often continue to consume camel meat.

Nutritive value. In comparison with medium-fat beef, camel meat has high levels of thiamine, riboflavin and iron, but low levels of fat and phosphorus (see Table 44).

CURED MEAT PRODUCTS
Pastirma or bastorma
Pastirma is a cured, dried meat known in Egypt, Lebanon, Jordan, Iraq and the Syrian Arab Republic. It is believed to have originated in Armenia or Turkey; the initial product, however, differed in some aspects to the one traditionally manufactured and consumed in Egypt and the Sudan. It is usually eaten at breakfast, especially with fried eggs. It is produced by numerous small plants, and manufacturers develop their own methods and

TABLE 44
Proximate gross composition and mineral content of camel meat
(value per 100 g edible portion)

Component	Value
Energy value *(kcal)*	193
Moisture *(g)*	72
Protein *(g)*	18.4
Lipids *(g)*	7.1
Ash *(g)*	0.9
Crude fibre *(g)*	0.2
Carbohydrates *(g)*	1.4
Calcium *(mg)*	5
Phosphorus *(mg)*	159
Iron *(mg)*	8.1

consider them a trade secret. Different brands, therefore, have different quality characteristics.

Preparation. The starting material for pastirma-processing is lean beef, often from older animals. The meat is deboned, and excess fat and fibrous and tough connective tissues are carefully removed. The meat is then cut, parallel to the fibres, into pieces of about 15-25 cm long, 5-10 cm wide and 3-5 cm thick, i.e. of oblong shape, being a little wider in the middle. The pieces of meat are slit by knife in several positions (about five to six positions, depending on the size of each piece) from one side to a depth of about half of the thickness of the meat. Each two pieces of meat are then tied together by a string from one end. The slits are then filled with the curing mixture (salted chilli), and the meat slices are pressed by hand and placed, one on top of the other with slits upwards, in wooden tanks in alternating layers with the curing mixture. The meat is left in this condition for ten to 20 hours, during which a salty fluid drains off. The meat slices are then

TABLE 45
Proximate gross composition of *pastirma*
(value per 100 g edible portion)

Component	Value
Energy value *(kcal)*	282
Moisture *(g)*	45
Protein *(g)*	21.5
Lipids *(g)*	14
Ash *(g)*	8.5
Crude fibre *(g)*	2
Carbohydrates *(g)*	9.5

rearranged by turning each one upside down and are left for another five to six hours, after which they are washed with water and sundried for about two days.

The sundried meat slices are then stacked in layers with the slit openings facing downwards, pressed by applying suitable weights on the top of a wooden board and left for eight to ten hours. The meat slices are then dried again in the sun for two to four days. Pressing followed by sundrying may be repeated till the product acquires the desired texture.

The surface of the partially dried meat slices is then rubbed strongly with the coating paste and then coated by a layer of the same paste about 1 cm in thickness. The coating paste consists of ground garlic, ground fenugreek seeds, ground dry paprika, flour and salt. Each manufacturer keeps the ingredients and their proportions as a trade secret; the quantities of fenugreek and flour, however, are usually three times as much as the rest of the other ingredients.

The product is then sundried for about three hours, and another coating layer is applied until the thickness of the coating reaches about 3-4 cm. Then the product is allowed to dry in the shade for one to two days, after which the pastirma is ripe and ready for marketing or storage. The whole process of manufacture lasts about three to four weeks.

For consumption, the pastirma is cut into slices of about 2-3 mm thick, and the coating is removed. Slices of pastirma could be eaten as such in sandwiches or fried, especially with eggs.

Nutritive value. Pastirma is rich in protein and energy and is an excellent source of minerals, particularly iron (see Table 45).

Kadide

Kadide is preserved lamb meat prepared in the Maghreb countries during the Islamic feast Aïd El Kebir. It is often used as an ingredient or flavouring agent in many preparations.

Preparation. This food is made from lamb or mutton and very seldom from beef or veal. Tail, legs, ribs and other fatty parts of the lamb are cut into thin strips to which the bones remain attached. These strips are rubbed with salt and crushed garlic in the proportions of 1kg of salt and 150 g of garlic for 7 kg of meat. The strips are then left for 24 hours. This first preservation step is followed by another rubbing with chilli powder, caraway, coriander and sometimes dry mint leaves. This seasoning, in addition to its preserving property, gives the product its typical taste. The meat is then suspended on horizontal ropes and exposed directly to sunlight for drying. This operation contributes to a partial dehydration, which reduces the chance for germ development and enhances the keeping quality of the product. When the meat is sufficiently dry but still tender, it is immersed in a mixture of boiling oil and melted fat for approximately 15 minutes, then stored in glass or earthen jars. The processes of salting, drying and boiling in oil are intended to stop and prevent germ development and proteolytic activity, resulting in higher preservation of the product. The keeping quality of the product is greatly increased if salting and drying are done properly and if strict hygiene is maintained during all processing steps.

For a comparison of the compositions of kadide, with and without oil, see Table 46.

TABLE 46
Proximate gross composition of *kadide*
(value per 100 g edible portion)

Component	*Kadide* with oil	*Kadide* without oil
Energy value *(kcal)*	508	426
Moisture *(g)*	33.4	41.6
Protein *(g)*	16.6	18.4
Lipids *(g)*	48.5	38.5
Carbohydrates *(g)*	-	-

Shermute

Shermute is typical of the Sudan and is composed of dry strips of meat usually cut into cylinders 20 cm long and about 1.5-2.5 cm in diameter. Traditionally, the meat strips are never dried in the direct sun. Drying always takes place indoors in places where there is good circulation of air currents. Drying therefore may take up to a week to be completed. During this process some thicker portions develop a proteolytic flavour. As a matter of fact, that portion in contact with the rope on which the strips are hung becomes both putrid and a little greenish.

In this traditional method, which dominates in the rural Sudan, the meat normally contains fat, which develops a rancid flavour during the drying process. The traditional shermute is therefore slightly fermented and has a characteristic flavour. It is sometimes consumed after barbecuing on burnt charcoal to make *shayya*. When it is extremely dry, some people eat it raw. Generally it is made into a sauce.

In urban communities, shermute is different: only lean, fat-free beef is used, the strips are very thin, and, they are sundried. This type of shermute is therefore almost unfermented and can simply be described as dry meat.

Research has shown that in the latter type of shermute, water activity of the meat drops from 0.99 to 0.94 in one day and to 0.60 in two days, thus

TABLE 47
Proximate gross composition of *naqaneq*
(value per 100 g edible portion)

Component	Value
Energy value *(kcal)*	508
Moisture *(g)*	20.9
Protein *(g)*	13.3
Lipids *(g)*	39.7
Ash *(g)*	3.8
Crude fibre *(g)*	0.8
Carbohydrates *(g)*	23.1

preventing growth of micro-organisms very quickly (microbes need a water activity of above 0.97). The most common bacteria in shermute were found to belong to the *Bacillus* and *Staphylococcus* genera.

SAUSAGES
Naqaneq
These sausages are prepared from low-grade beef, pork or mutton meat, usually flavoured with spices and wines. They are usually heated on direct fire or fried in their own juice before consumption.

Preparation. The meat to be prepared into sausages is usually rich in animal fat. It is well minced and then mixed with the following spices: pepper, nutmeg, cloves, coriander and ginger. About 50 g of the spice mix is used per kilogram of meat. This mixture is allowed to cure for several hours to two days, depending on the temperature. Sometimes a binder in the form of corn (maize) flour is added. Salt and vinegar are also added at the rates of 2 percent each before filling the meat into a natural casing. The casing is prepared from washed sheep intestine and, with the help of a funnel-like

extruder, the casing is filled with the meat to make short links. The sausages are then hung to dry for several hours at room temperature.
For the nutrient content of naqaneq, see Table 47.

Sujuk

Sujuk is a sausage that has a strong characteristic flavour and is brick-red in colour. It is based on beef meat and was originally introduced by the Armenian communities of the Near East but is now widely consumed by various peoples of the area.

Preparation. Like many other sausages, the basic steps involved in the preparation of sujuk include mincing of fatty meat and addition of spices before stuffing the mix into convenient edible envelopes. In the formulation of sujuk, spices make up 5-6 percent of the meat weight, with cumin and red pepper as the major ingredients. The minced meat and spices are well mixed and then filled into casings made from beef intestine. Small holes are perforated in the casing, and knots are tied every 10-15 cm. The sausages are then subjected to pressure for a prolonged period of time to allow the liquid to drain and evaporate. As a result of the pressure, the sausages acquire a flattened crescent shape and retain a dark, brick-red colour. It is believed that the high concentration of spices along with the dehydration process of the meat allow storage of the sausages in the open air without need of refrigeration.

A typical recipe is as follows:
 10 kg of beef with 40-50 percent fat, minced fine
 200 g cumin
 100 g allspice
 50 g black pepper
 150 g ground cinnamon
 150 g red pepper

Iraqi *bastirma*

Iraqi *bastirma* sausage is a spiced, fermented and salted sausage that is commonly consumed in Iraq, especially during the winter months. It is usually consumed after boiling on direct fire or after frying in its own fat.

Preparation. Lean meat from beef or sheep is used in the preparation of bastirma sausage. Whatever the source of lean meat is, it is usually mixed with sheep-tail fat in the proportion of 3 parts meat to 1 part fat. The fat imparts a special flavour and modifies the texture of the final product. The fat-meat mixture is ground to a fine homogeneous mass, and salt, minced garlic and spices are added. The spice mix used gives Iraqi bastirma its characteristic taste; it is prepared according to the following formula:

Ingredient	Rate of addition %
Black pepper	25
Cinnamon	17
Cumin	9
Ginger	7
Rose petals	6
Ginger stem	6
Allspice	6
Red pepper	6
Coriander	3
Cardamom	2
Cloves	2

The spiced meat is then thoroughly mixed and stuffed in casings of sheep intestine. The sausages are then pressed into a flat shape by holding them under a weight of 2-5 kg (depending on the amount of sausages weighing 0.5-1 kg) for one day. The flat, crescent-shaped sausages are suspended from ceilings in the open air for several hours for a final curing until the outer skin is fairly dry.

Nutritive value. Iraqi bastirma sausages have the following composition per 100 g edible portion:
- Energy value *(kcal)*   306-382
- Moisture   50-55
- Protein   12-15
- Lipids   28-35
- Ash   2.5-3

Merguez

This type of sausage is made of ground meat and fat (most often lamb), filled into natural casing. The sausage can be used fresh, but Tunisians prefer it dried and immersed in olive oil and stored. Similar products are made in Spain in the form of *olla* preserves, using pork instead of lamb and beef.

Preparation. Meat and fat are finely ground and mixed in a proportion of 2:1. The ground meat is dressed with salt, cinnamon, black pepper, harissa (see p. 117), powdered, dry mint leaves and rose blossoms. The seasoned meat and fat are introduced with the aid of special equipment into casings prepared from washed lamb intestine. The filled intestine is tied at equal distances of ten centimetres to make a separation between the pieces of *merguez*. The strips of merguez are then suspended on a horizontal rope for sundrying. It is necessary to make fine holes in the intestine while drying is taking place. The holes allow for moisture, air and excess melted fats to come out so that the drying step is speeded up. After dehydration, the product is immersed in boiled oil for 15 minutes, then stored in glass jars covered with the same cooked oil.

This heat treatment is important for the preservation of merguez. If merguez is prepared to be eaten immediately, this step is usually avoided. Merguez enters into many preparations (couscous, stews, bazine) or can be grilled or fried and consumed with bread.

Merguez, made generally from beef, is now prepared and sold by most butchers. A certain number of problems are associated with the traditional processing. The risk of contamination is high in handling such very perishable goods as meat and meat products, particularly when proper

TABLE 48
Proximate gross composition of fresh and dried *merguez*
(value per 100 g, dry-weight basis)

Component	Fresh *merguez*	Dried *merguez*
Energy value *(kcal)*	243	554
Moisture *(g)*	62.8	17.1
Protein *(g)*	16.4	37.4
Lipids *(g)*	19.1	43.6
Carbohydrates *(g)*	0.2	0.4

hygienic conditions are lacking. There is no rigorous control of the quality, composition and grading of this product. The use of prohibited flavouring or colouring agents has been reported many times. It is clear then that the production, marketing and control of this product suffer from many weaknesses that must be resolved if good quality merguez is to be promoted.

For an analysis of the compositions of fresh and dried merguez see Table 48.

OTHER MEAT PRODUCTS
Lakhliâa
Lakhliâa is commonly used in all parts of Morocco as an ingredient for many preparations (couscous, mhammas, stews, etc.) or as a snack with eggs and bread. It is dried meat that has been immersed in a mixture of animal fat and oil to improve its keeping quality. The characteristic taste of the product is highly appreciated by consumers. Lakhliâa is similar to kadide in Tunisia and to a product of the same name in Algeria.

Preparation. Kadide is first prepared as described earlier and then immersed in a mixture of boiling fat and oil made of 2 litres of olive oil and 2 kg melted sheep-tail fat. Lakhliâa's characteristic taste and smell are produced during this process. The product is then stored in large earthenware jars.

TABLE 49
Proximate gross composition of *lakhliâa*
(value per 100 g edible portion)

Component	Value
Energy value *(kcal)*	720
Moisture *(g)*	6.7
Protein *(g)*	7
Lipids *(g)*	74
Ash *(g)*	0.7
Crude fibre *(g)*	2.5
Carbohydrates *(g)*	7.1

Lakhliâa is used in various ways. It is a major ingredient of the filling for rghaief (see p. 27). It is also used as a fat component in various preparations: vegetable stews, couscous, mhammas, etc. Lakhliâa is traditionally prepared during the Islamic feast of Aïd El Idha, but it is also prepared on other occasions (weddings, celebrations of important events, etc.). It can also be prepared independently of any special event just to renew or increase the annual supply. Lakhliâa is produced and marketed on a very small scale by traditional food dealers. Given its desired taste and its good keeping quality, this product has a good potential of being prepared industrially for commercial marketing.

Nutritive value. The values presented in Table 49 were calculated by the author based on the recipe and the actual quantities of ingredients provided by a reliable informant.

Qawarma

Qawarma is a way to preserve meat without refrigeration for long periods of time. It is used in all the countries of the Near East where sheep are abundant and is often prepared in summer for use in winter.

TABLE 50
Proximate gross composition of *qawarma*
(value per 100 g edible portion)

Component	Value
Energy value *(kcal)*	702
Moisture *(g)*	5.5
Protein *(g)*	20
Lipids *(g)*	65.5
Ash *(g)*	4
Carbohydrates *(g)*	5

Preparation. The kind of sheep that is raised in the Near East has a huge fat tail. This makes it ideal for the preparation of qawarma which consists of small pieces of red meat dehydrated by frying and submerged in solidified fat. The ratio of red meat to tail is usually 1:2. The red meat is cut into small pieces about 2 x 2 cm and heavily salted (5 percent w/w). The meat is left overnight in a cool place until it turns grey in colour. The flavour develops during this period, and the meat is fried in its own juice with very little water if any added, until it is well done. In a separate container, the fat is divided into small pieces to facilitate its melting when put over a low fire. The fat is heated slowly until it melts, and heating is continued until all the moisture is driven out. Salt and spices are added, and the fried red meat is added to the molten fat. The sterile meat, which is salted and surrounded by very dry fat, stores quite well for long periods of time. Qawarma is usually used as a source of fat and meat in frying eggs or in the preparation of kishk-based breakfast meals (see p. 60).

Nutritive value. Qawarma is a rich source of proteins and very rich source of calories (see Table 50).

FERMENTED FISH

Feseekh

Feseekh is a traditional, salt-fermented fish, quite popular in many parts of the Arab countries. Processors of feseekh have their own procedures of salting that are handed down from father to son and considered to be a trade secret, and hence the finished product differs greatly in quality and acceptability from one processor to the next. The characteristic sharp, penetrating odour of salted fish permeates the air in and around the processing site. Preparation of feseekh is believed to be a pickling process, coupled with putrifactive fermentation in which micro-organisms, associated with native fish enzymes, play a major role during processing and ripening.

Preparation. Feseekh is prepared by salting partially fermented whole mullet *(Mugil cephalus)* and ageing it for a period of time that depends on the salt concentration. In the Sudan, other kinds of fish are also used, such as *Hydrocynus* sp., *Alestes* sp. and *Petrocephalus* sp.

According to the traditional method, which is actually a combination of dry and wet salting, the fish is left to ferment in the sun for one to two days, during which it partially swells. The fish is then dry salted in barrels or vats using granular salt. The salting process involves stuffing the gills and placing the fish in layers alternating with granular salt. It is then pressed down by putting suitable weights on the top and leaving it for about two days. The amount of salt used is about 20 percent of the weight of the fish. The brine formed during this time as a result of the osmotic pressure is supplemented by the addition of saturated brine to completely cover the fish. The fish is then allowed to cure for a suitable period of time ranging from one week to two months.

On the basis of salt concentration and the period of curing, there are two types of feseekh: sweet feseekh (lightly salted, 10-15 percent) and salty feseekh (heavily salted, 20-25 percent). During the curing period, the fish undergoes certain characteristic changes in which bacteria and native fish enzymes are involved and develop the flavour and the sharp, penetrating odour characteristic to feseekh.

TABLE 51
Proximate gross composition of *feseekh*
(value per 100 g, wet-weight basis)

Component	Salty *feseekh*	Sweet *feseekh*
Energy value *(kcal)*	153	109
Moisture *(g)*	51.6	58
Protein *(g)*	22.5	21
Lipids *(ether extract) (g)*	7	6.3
Salt *(g)*	18.7	15.7
Ash *(g)*	1.7	1.1

Sweet feseekh has a sharp odour and a mild, salty and rather acidic taste. It has a reddish flesh colour and a soft texture. The outer skin is golden yellow in colour. Salty feseekh has a distinctive sharp aroma with a strong, salty and rather acidic taste. The flesh is reddish with a rather soft texture. The skin is golden yellow in colour.

Feseekh is not packed in special containers and is usually supplied to the market in the processing barrel.

For a comparison of the nutritive value of salty and sweet feseekh, see Table 51.

Mehiawah

Mehiawah, a fermented fish sauce, was introduced by Iranian immigrants to the Arabian Gulf countries and has become since then one of the traditional foods of Bahrain, Qatar, Kuwait and the United Arab Emirates. Mehiawah is usually prepared at home, but is now available at some local bakeries that produce tanoor bread. The quantities prepared for marketing are small and depend mainly on home preparation.

Preparation. Mehiawah is prepared from a mixture of tiny, pickled fish (Indian oil sardines), water, spices and salt. The fish are cleaned and washed

TABLE 52
Proximate gross composition of *mehiawah*
(value per 100 g edible portion)

Component	Value
Energy value *(kcal)*	113
Moisture *(g)*	67.6
Protein *(g)*	8
Lipids *(g)*	2.6
Ash *(g)*	5.5
Crude fibre *(g)*	1.8
Carbohydrates *(g)*	14.5

thoroughly and racked in glass bottles filled with brine. The bottles are then tightly covered and put in sunlight for seven to 15 days for fermentation. The fermented fish are then mashed and strained. A special mixture of spices is roasted, ground and mixed with the fermented fish. The mixture is preserved in glass bottles for further fermentation for five to ten days.

Mehiawah is generally spread on tanoor bread, then folded or rolled and served with spring onions. It is a preferred food for breakfast.

Nutritive value. The composition (see Table 52) of mehiawah varies considerably, depending on the amount of fish used and water added. Since mehiawah is usually very salty, it is consumed in small quantities. Generally, one to two tablespoons of mehiawah are spread over one tanoor bread.

Tareeh

Tareeh, like mehiawah (see above section), is prepared from fermented fish, but it is more concentrated. It is limited to house preparation and is rarely available on the market.

TABLE 53
Proximate gross composition and mineral content of *tareeh*
(value per 100 g edible portion)

Component	Value
Energy value *(kcal)*	80
Moisture *(g)*	58.5
Protein *(g)*	14.9
Lipids *(g)*	1.8
Ash *(g)*	23.2
Crude fibre *(g)*	0.5
Carbohydrates *(g)*	1.1
Calcium *(mg)*	525
Phosphorus *(mg)*	473
Iron *(mg)*	3
Sodium *(mg)*	4204
Zinc *(mg)*	161.5

Preparation. Tareeh consists of fish, salt, cumin, and red chillies. The fish (Indian oil sardines) are washed, drained and mixed with salt, cumin and red chillies. The mixture is then put into a big container and kept in sunlight for one week, or until the fish are soft. Just before consumption, the tareeh is diluted with water as required and eaten with bread, spring onions, and radish leaves.

Table 53 illustrates the composition and mineral content of tareeh.

DRIED FISH
Samak or mujaffaf

Drying is one of the traditional methods for the preservation of fish in the Gulf. The fish is salted and spread under sunlight for three to seven days, depending on the kind of fish. Shrimps, small sardines and sharks are commonly used for dehydration. Salted, dried fish is used for the preparation of some traditional foods such as mehiawah, tareeh and stews.

TABLE 54
Proximate gross composition and mineral content of some fish consumed in the Arabian Gulf (value per 100 g edible portion)

Component	Crab (gubgub)	Grouper (hamour)	Mullet (maid)	Sea bream (muchawah)	Shrimp, dried (nubian)	Shrimp, raw (nubian)
Energy value (kcal)	57	107	183	148	331	85
Moisture (g)	85.8	76.4	67.3	70.4	8.1	78.1
Protein (g)	11.4	18.8	18.6	19	76.4	17.8
Lipids (g) (crude ether extract)	0.7	3.6	12.1	8	1.2	0.9
Ash (g)	2	1.1	1.9	2.5	10.5	1.6
Crude fibre (g)	-	-	-	-	-	-
Carbohydrates (g)	0.5	-	-	-	3.9	1.5
Calcium (mg)	-	18	339	512	1158	164
Phosphorus (mg)	-	210	367	433	969	276
Iron (mg)	-	0.64	1.74	1.65	62	2.61

Crabs *(gubgub)* comprise another seafood commonly consumed in the Gulf. Crabs are boiled in salted water until well done. The flesh is then eaten along with salads.

Nutritive value. In general, fish is rich in protein. Dried fish is very high in protein, due to its low moisture content. Some fish are rich in fat content such as *maid* (12.1 percent), *muchawah* (7.8 percent), and *zobaidy* (6.7 percent). Iron and phosphorus contents are high in dried fish as is the content of sodium, which makes it not suitable for hypertensive people.

It is well documented that fish has a preventive effect on coronary heart diseases, which are the main cause of death in the Gulf. The effect of fish on such diseases is attributed to its content of omega-3 fatty acids, which are believed to lower the cholesterol level in blood.

For the proximate and mineral composition of some fish commonly consumed in the Gulf, see Table 54.

TABLE 55
Proximate gross composition and mineral content of salted sardines
(value per 100 g, wet-weight basis)

Component	Value
Energy value *(kcal)*	250
Moisture *(g)*	47.5
Protein *(g)*	25.3
Lipids *(ether extract)* *(g)*	16.6
Ash *(g)*	16
Calcium *(mg)*	0.5
Phosphorus *(mg)*	0.5
Sodium chloride *(mg)*	13.5

BRINED FISH
Salted sardines

Preparation. Sardines *(Sardinella eba, S. aurita)* are dry salted on commercial scale by placing freshly caught fish in alternating layers with granular salt in watertight vats or barrels. The layers of fish are then pressed down by putting suitable weights on the top that keep the fish totally submerged under the formed brine. A reasonable quantity of granular dry salt is placed first at the bottom of the container, and a bigger quantity is placed in a thicker layer on the top. The salt used is about 20-40 percent of the weight of the fish. Sardines usually mature within one to two weeks and can be kept without spoilage as such for a few months, depending on the brine concentration. Some families salt sardines for their own needs with a lower proportion of salt (15-20 percent), and hence the maturation period as well as the shelf-life are shorter.

For the nutrient content of salted sardines, see Table 55.

TABLE 56
Proximate gross composition and nutritive value of *melouha*
(value per 100 g, dry-weight basis)

Component	Fresh	Dry salting	Pickling
Energy value *(kcal)*	485.7	422.5	217.8
Moisture *(g)*	76.4	52.3	58.6
Sodium chloride *(g)*	0.2	34.4	49.7
Total protein *(g)*	73	47.3	35.3
Crude fat *(g)*	21.5	12.5	8.4
Total ash *(g)*	4.4	37.9	55.6
Calcium *(mg)*	186.8	-	815.9
Iron *(mg)*	4.9	-	14.1
Phosphorus *(mg)*	269.03	-	126.9

Melouha

Melouha is a salted fish produced and consumed traditionally in Egypt and the Sudan. It has a characteristic, appetite-stimulating flavour.

Preparation. The traditional starting material for melouha is a fish called *kalb el-samak (Hydrocynus forskalii)*. Its high edible portion (81 percent) makes it suitable for melouha processing. The salting process is carried out in two stages. In the first, freshly caught fish are placed in alternative layers with granular salt in a wicker bag made of palm tree leaves to facilitate drainage of liquids. Salt is used at the level of 10 percent of the weight of the fish. The second stage starts about 24 hours after all the free liquid is separated and drained off. The dry fish are then transferred to another container, usually tins of about 20-kg capacity, or barrels, and arranged as in the first stage in alternating layers with granular salt (about 20 percent of the original weight of the fish). After a period of 45 days, saturated salt solution is added to the top to completely cover the fish. Salting is complete, and melouha becomes ripe after a total of about 120 days. The fish may be eviscerated before salting. During the salting (pickling) and the aging period, the fish acquire a strong salty taste and a characteristic aroma attributed to the enzymatic formation of glutamic acid.

Melouha is not packed in special containers and usually sold as such in the packing barrels.

Nutritive value. As a result of salting kalb el-samak for 120 days, the moisture content decreases by 23.5 percent. Phosphorus and total amino-acids decrease, while salt, total ash, total protein, calcium and iron contents increase (see Table 56).

Bibliography

Ahmed, H.S. 1975. *Chemical studies on fish preservation in Egypt with special reference to its nutritive value.* Dept Food Science and Technology, Faculty of Agriculture, Univ. Cairo. (M.Sc. thesis)

El-Sharnouby, S.A., Aman, M. El-Bastawisy & Mousa, M. 1988. *The role of enzymes in determining the quality of salted and cured fish.* Dept Food Science and Technology, Faculty of Agriculture, Univ. Alexandria. (Ph.D. thesis)

Faraj, E. 1984. *Human nutrition in health and disease – Maktabat Al Nahdah Al Masriyah,* p. 124. Cairo, Egypt. (in Arabic)

Hubert, A. 1984. *Le pain et l'olive: aspects de l'alimentation en Tunisie.* Centre régional de publication. Lyons, Editions du CNRS.

INS. 1975. *Table de composition des aliments tunisiens.* Institut national de la statistique. Claude Jardin, FAO Consultant, Tunis.

Kouki, M. 1967. *La cuisine tunisienne "d'Ommok Sannafa".* Tunis, SAEP.

Musaiger, A.O. 1988. *The situation of fisheries in Bahrain,* p. 34-436. Bahrain, Al-Yamani Commercial and Management Services Bureau.

Pellett, P.L. & Shadarevian, S. 1970. *Food composition tables for use in the Middle East,* p. 23. Beirut, Lebanon, American University of Beirut Press.

Rashad, F.M. 1986. *Bacteriological and chemical studies on salted mullet fish "Feseekh": a traditional fermented fish product in Egypt.* Dept Agric. Microbiology, Faculty of Agriculture, Univ. Cairo. (Ph.D. thesis)

Salama, M. El-Sayed. 1969. *Chemical and technological studies on Egyptian salted sardines.* Dept Food Science and Technology, Faculty of Agriculture, Univ. Alexandria. (M.Sc. thesis)

Shahine, A.B. 1965. *Chemical composition of salted fermented fish "Feseekh" at various stages of fermentation.* Dept Food Science, Faculty of Agriculture, Univ. Cairo. (M.Sc. thesis)

Taha, M.E.A.A. 1966. *Chemical and technological studies on "Pastirma"*. Dept Food Science and Technology, Faculty of Agriculture, Univ. Alexandria. (M.Sc. thesis)

Teutscher, F. 1988. *Small pelagics and health*. INFOSAMAK fact sheet No. 22788. Bahrain.

Chapter 4
Fruits and vegetables

FRUITS
Dates and date products
Date palms (*Phoenix dactylifera*) are the most extensively cultivated fruit tree in the countries of the Near East. The tree was cultivated as far back as 400 BC in southern Iraq. The present annual production of Saudi Arabia alone is more than 500 000 tonnes per year.

The tree itself provides shade and comfort for desert dwellers, while its trunk can be used to build doors and fences. Its fronds are used for fuel, and the leaflets are woven into mats and baskets used to pack the ripe fruit. The fruit itself is an excellent source of energy and, if properly processed, can be stored for a very long time. A major portion of the harvest is allowed to ripen on the tree to the *tamer* stage and then packed directly in straw boxes. Sometimes, the fruit is sundried before storage, but such treatment exposes the fruit to insect infestation.

Efforts to develop new foods from dates are going on in Iraq, Saudi Arabia, Egypt and other countries of the Near East. Among the traditional foods that are derived from the date palm are ripened dates, date syrup and date preserves. New foods based on dates are constantly being developed, such as *tamrina* (a weaning food developed in Iraq), *tamreddine* (a thin sheet of fruit prepared by dehydrating a date extract, developed in Saudi Arabia) and candy bars based on date paste.

Preparation
Date preserves. Large fruits are preferred for the preparation of preserves because of their attractive appearance and easier handling during peeling, pitting and stuffing operations. The fruits are washed, dried and then peeled. Care should be taken to remove only the peel, which is rich in astringent

compounds, and not the underlying pulp, which is sweet and has a pleasant flavour. The peeled fruits are then boiled in water until they become soft. This softening of the fruit facilitates removal of the pit and its replacement with a roasted almond. A sugar syrup is prepared by boiling a sugar-water solution in a ratio of 2:1 (w/w) and placing the stuffed dates in the boiling syrup until well cooked. The end point is marked by the disappearance of evolving water vapour from the cooking mix. The cooked dates are filled hot into glass jars with airtight twist-off caps.

Ripened dates. Date fruits, when harvested from the palm tree, have a strongly astringent taste. Their quality can be greatly improved by allowing them a ripening period, during which many changes occur in the texture and taste of the fruit. Ripening can occur when the fruits are still on the branches or if individually removed for cleaning and fumigation before ripening.

A special room maintained at about 35°C for a few days is necessary to allow enzymatic changes to occur in the fruit. Sprinkling the fruits with a very light mist of olive oil mixed with vinegar may help the ripening process. During this time, the dates become soft and translucent. The aroma improves considerably, and all traces of astringency disappear. Most important is the transformation that occurs in the sugars, in which most of the sucrose is changed to invert sugar, causing a considerable increase in the juiciness and sweetness of the fruit. The ripened dates, often with the pits removed, are then packed and pressed into palm-leaf baskets, large cans or small cellophane packages.

Dates are now commercially produced in different ways. *Tamer*-stage dates, sometimes mixed with nuts, are available in metal or plastic containers. Frozen dates at *rutab* stage are also available on the market. Dates are sometimes mixed with *tehineh* and sold as a confection. Commercially, dates can also be utilized in the manufacture of date syrup. The stones of dates are not usually used for human consumption, but are separated, ground and sold as animal feed.

Nutritive value. Dates are considered a very good source of energy and a fair source of minerals. *Rzaiz tamr* was reported to have the following composition per 100 g edible material:

- Energy value *(kcal)*   383
- Moisture   8.7
- Protein   2.8
- Reducing sugars   77.5
- Total sugars   82.4
- Ash   1.3

Date syrup. Large quantities of surplus dates are often used to extract date syrup, or *dibbs*, or they may be dried and used later for consumption. The traditional method for the extraction of date syrup is carried out by placing the dates in a small room of 1-2 m high. The room is built with a slanting floor, which is covered by a thick mat made from date-palm leaves. The dates are spread on the mat in layers until they almost reach the roof of the room. The upper layer of dates is then covered by another layer of mats. This method of stacking the dates causes a rise in their temperature because of the slow fermentative activity that takes place. These conditions cause the date syrup to flow onto the ground and run through a small hole into a container. Commercially, this method is not practical, as only 15 percent of the syrup can be extracted. Nowadays, there is a mechanical method for the extraction of date syrup, in which a hydraulic press can efficiently extract a greater proportion of the date sugars and other soluble solids. Date syrup is used in the preparation of many traditional foods and dishes, such as date bread, *legaimat* (doughnut cake) and *mahmer* (sweet rice).

Grape products

Raisins. The production of raisins remains a family activity and is always done on a limited scale, because most of the varieties of grape that are under cultivation in the area are seeded with a firm pulp and moderate to tough skin; they are suitable only for table use and unfit for raisin production.

Preparation. Fine sawdust, sifted free of debris, is added to water at a rate of one cup per 4.5 litres. The water is heated, and a small amount of olive oil is added. When the solution becomes hot, grape clusters are dipped in it for a short period of time before they are placed in trays in the sun to dry. The sawdust makes the solution alkaline (pH 8-9), which causes very small fissures in the grape skin when the grape clusters are dipped in the boiling solution. The fissures speed the drying process, resulting in an improved colour and texture. The oil, which floats at the surface of the boiling liquid, causes the formation of a thin film that coats individual berries, preventing them from becoming hard and sticky. The residue of the sawdust that remains after drying gives the raisins a dirty appearance; therefore it is desirable if the oil is not added to the sawdust suspension, but rather a second hot oil-water dip is given to the dried clusters. This quick dip serves to clean the berries, freeing them of insect eggs and other contaminants, and to pasteurize them. A second dehydration, which is usually very short (a few hours), is enough to dry the clean raisins and get them ready for consumption.

Although sawdust is a product of wood combustion at high temperature and is itself considered sterile if properly handled, the residue it leaves on the fruits gives them an undesirable appearance. Caustic soda can be safely used to prepare the lye solution. If soda-oil dip is used, a second immediate dip in cold water can be employed to wash any hydroxide residue off of the berries. The second water dip can contain a metabisulfite salt as a source of SO_2, or the dehydration can be performed in a stream of hot sulphur fumes. The sulphur helps the disinfecting process and prevents the browning of the raisins, so that the final product is golden yellow in colour.

Nutritive value. Raisins are mainly consumed along with other foods to give a sweet, fruity flavour. Because they are a concentrated source of sugar, they are considered very rich in energy. Raisins also contain a considerable amount of iron.

Grape molasses. Excess grapes that are not harvested for table use are left on the vine to become ripe and may be used for the production of molasses. Grape varieties that bear white, soft berries that are rich in juice are preferred. The sugar content should be high and the acid content very low. Preparing molasses from grape juice is one way of preserving the value of the fruit for winter use. The high concentration of sugar in the final product provides preservative action. Care should be taken not to allow yeast or mould to contaminate this food, as they have been known to survive to some extent on this medium.

Preparation. The grapes are usually washed free of dust and dirt and exposed to the sun to dry. The berries are then crushed and pressed to release the juice. The collected juice is filtered free of seeds and skins and then subjected to prolonged heating with continuous stirring, until a noticeable increase in its viscosity is obtained. During heating, the froth that forms on the surface is skimmed off, and a small amount of washed and dried clay powder is added. The juice is allowed to settle overnight, and the clear supernatant is collected separately and heated again. Heating is discontinued when the syrup becomes viscous, as evidenced by the change in the spattering pattern of the bubbles. The molasses is then stored in glass or clay jars. Air may be incorporated in the cooled molasses by continuous fast beating with a wooden stick. The air bubbles incorporated by this continuous beating impart to the molasses a lighter colour and a thicker consistency.

This food is considered a delicatessen speciality, and its processing details should be standardized as to the total-solids content, viscosity specifications and sugar or acid content of the raw material.

Nutritive value. Grape molasses are prepared by concentrating grape juice; they therefore have a high carbohydrate content and some vegetable fats and proteins. The mineral content, particularly that of iron, may be significant, and the undigested residue is low compared to other fruit products.

Malban. A soft candy made from wheat starch and concentrated grape juice, it is essentially a source of energy and, like other sweets, is very low in its nutritive value.

Preparation. Grape juice is boiled in the presence of some clarifying agent (clay is used successfully). The boiling is carried out to concentrate the juice until the final sugar concentration in the clear liquid reaches 37-40 percent.

Powdered wheat starch, at the rate of 10 percent (w/v) is added to the concentrated grape juice, and the mixture is cooked above a low fire with constant stirring, until complete gelatinization of the starch is obtained. The hot slurry is then flavoured with rose water and orange-blossom water (see p. 148), and poured in flat trays in layers 4 cm thick. Pistachio nuts, almonds or wild pine nuts are frequently added to the cooked mix. When the mixture develops a hard-gel consistency, it is allowed to dry well on both sides. The solid mass is then cut into small cubes and dusted with powdered wheat starch to prevent the pieces from adhering to each other. It may then be wrapped in cellophane for storage.

Carob

Carob molasses. *Dibbs el kharoub*, or carob molasses, is a viscous, dark syrup extracted from carob-bean pods. The carob tree *Ceratonia siliqua* is a hardy evergreen tree that grows in dry areas of the Mediterranean region and attains great height and size with age.

Preparation. The pods are harvested in late summer and collected at a special stone mill for grinding. Grinding causes pulverization of all the contents of the pods except the seeds, which are very hard and can be separated from the ground mass. The powdered carobs can be stored as such for several months at room temperature or used immediately to extract the sweet molasses. Extraction starts by soaking the powdered carobs in water for a period of one or two days, until the sugary material dissolves. The unextracted residue is used as a feed for animals or as a soil conditioner. The seeds are separated and usually exported to industrialized countries to be used as a source of locust bean gum. The extract is further clarified by additional filtration until it becomes a clear solution. The clear syrup is then concentrated in special kettles that are heated to a very high temperature. The cooled and concentrated syrup is usually filled in plastic containers and stored for long periods of time without any refrigeration.

Nutritive value. The analysis of this food reflects its extremely high content of food energy that comes from its high carbohydrate content (see Table 57).

Carob drink. The fruit of the tree *Ceratonia siliqua* L., which is known in Egypt, the Sudan and the Arab countries as *kharrub*, has been known in Egypt since the ancient Egyptians, who used it as food and feed as well as for medicinal purposes.

Nowadays, carob pods constitute a popular food in Egypt, the Sudan and many of the Arab countries, where the pods are consumed either as such, especially during the fasting month of Ramadan, or for preparing a summer soft drink.

Preparation. Carob drink is prepared by extracting whole or crushed pods in water. It is then sweetened with sugar and served as a cold drink. There are different methods for extraction, the most commonly used of which starts by soaking cleaned and crushed pods in water overnight. The mixture is then

TABLE 57
Proximate gross composition of carob molasses
(value per 100 g edible portion)

Component	Value
Energy value *(kcal)*	293
Moisture *(g)*	21.2
Protein *(g)*	–
Lipids *(crude ether extract) (g)*	0.1
Ash *(g)*	7.7
Crude fibre *(g)*	0.4
Nitrogen-free extract *(g)*	70.6

brought to boiling and held at this temperature for a few minutes. Too much boiling affects the characteristic flavour and aroma of the carob. The mixture is then filtered through muslin cloth and sweetened to taste. The colour is usually adjusted by the addition of caramel colour. Cold extraction yields a dark-yellowish-coloured extract of good flavour but low sweetness. Hot extraction below boiling temperature (96°C) yields an extract of dark-brownish colour and good odour, but slightly astringent taste. Prolonged boiling yields a dark-brownish extract, with natural odour, but distinct astringent taste.

Carob extract may also be prepared by mixing clean and crushed pods with a suitable quantity of sucrose; the mixture is heated for a few minutes, after which a suitable volume of hot water is added. The whole mixture is heated again to boiling and kept at boiling temperature for about four minutes. It is then filtered through muslin cloth. The resulting extract is characterized by a good flavour and a popular colour similar to the natural colour of the pods.

Experimental research has been carried out, aimed at the preparation of a concentrate from carob extract to be utilized in the preparation of soft drinks and carbonated beverages.

TABLE 58
Proximate gross composition and nutritive value of carob pods (value per 100 g edible portion, dry-weight basis)

Component	Value
Energy value *(kcal)*	233.5
Moisture *(g)*	12.5
Total insoluble solids *(g)*	33.7
Total soluble solids *(g)*	66.2
Reducing sugars *(g)*	12.4
Glucose *(g)*	2.5
Fructose *(g)*	9.9
Sucrose *(g)*	33.7
Acid hydrolysable polysaccharides *(g)*	5.6
Cellulose and hemicellulose *(g)*	20.2
Crude fibres *(g)*	5.7
Protein *(g)*	4
Ether extract *(g)*	1
Acidity as citric acid *(g)*	1.5

Nutritive value. Carob pods have a high carbohydrate content (more than 60 percent on wet-weight basis), nearly half of which is sucrose, which represents about 50 percent of the total soluble-solids content. Their composition is illustrated in Table 58.

Pomegranate extract

This strong acidulate is extracted from the fruits of a sour variety of *Punica granatum*. It is used particularly with meat pies and dishes containing meat. It is actually a very concentrated juice prepared in the form of a thick syrup, very rich in red pigments. It imparts a delicate flavour along with a pleasing sour taste to food.

Preparation. A variety of pomegranates that have very sour fruit is used. The fruit should not be allowed to become overripe because its acidity decreases. The peels of pomegranate fruit must be removed completely before pressing the juice out. Any residue of the peels imparts to the juice a marked tartness because of the peels' high content of phenolic compounds and tannic acid, which coagulate the mucoproteins of the mouth and cause the astringency.

The clean fruits are pressed to free the juice, which is bright pink in colour. The juice is filtered free of seeds and boiled slowly in an open kettle until it becomes viscous. Before the boiling is terminated, 5 percent of sodium chloride is added to the concentrated solution, which is allowed to cool before being filled into glass bottles. The addition of salt to the resulting syrup softens the sharp, sour taste of the juice and contributes to the preservative effect of the soluble solids; otherwise, yeasts and mould may grow on the carbohydrates that are present in the syrup.

It is evident that preparation of the concentrated syrup requires prolonged boiling, which causes some changes in the flavour and colour of the final product. Vacuum concentration, at least in the early stage of boiling, may reduce the damages caused by excessive heating and result in better flavour and colour in the final product.

Quamareddeen

Quamareddeen is a favourite dried-fruit product that is consumed generally during the winter months and is particularly popular during the fast of Ramadan. It is usually available as a thin, flat, yellow-orange sheet of dried fruit pulp with a sweet-sourish taste. It is produced mainly in such apricot-producing countries as the Syrian Arab Republic and Lebanon.

Preparation. The preparation of quamareddeen is still carried out on a small scale from overripe apricot fruit. The fruits are blanched, then mashed and strained through a coarse sieve (a straw basket is generally used) to separate the seeds and skin from the pulp and juice. The thick syrupy juice is collected

TABLE 59
Proximate gross composition of *quamareddeen*
(value per 100 g edible portion)

Component	Value
Energy value *(kcal)*	338
Moisture *(g)*	14 (ranges from 10–25)
Protein *(g)*	2
Lipids *(crude ether extract) (g)*	2
Ash *(g)*	3.4
Carbohydrates *(g)*	78

in wooden trays, which are thoroughly oiled prior to use. Metal containers cannot be used because of the high acid content of the fruit. Stainless steel trays may be used, but wood is preferred because of its lower cost. The oil coating of the wood helps prevent the adherence of the pulp to the wood during the drying procedure and reduces the absorption by the wood of the juice and its flavour components. The thickness of the strained apricot mash in these trays is usually less than 1 cm at the start of the drying step. Dehydration is carried out in the sun for a period of approximately 20 days, depending on the weather conditions. The final product is a thin, continuous film, slightly elastic, 1-2 mm thick, and is usually wrapped in yellow cellophane sheets and stored at room temperature. It is often consumed as such without reconstitution.

Nutritive value. Quamareddeen contains a considerable amount of plant fibre and pectin, but its main feature is its high energy content. It is equally well accepted by young and old. Table 59 illustrates its composition.

Citrus products

Rough lemon preserve. Rough lemon (*Citrus aurantium*) is a citrus tree that is usually used as a rootstock for grafting oranges and lemons. When the ungrafted tree is allowed to grow to maturity, it bears large fruits that have a thick, rough outside peel and a strong flavour. No part of the fruit is accepted as readily edible. The thick peel can serve as a raw material for the production of a special preserve that has an attractive yellow colour and a characteristic flavour.

Preparation. Fruits that have a thick but smooth peel are preferred. The flavedo, the outermost yellow layer of cells, is partially removed by abrasion. Most of the oil glands that are responsible for the strong flavour and bitter taste of the peel are found in this layer. A faint residual yellow colour is intentionally retained, and the fruits are cut to facilitate separation of the peel from the carpels, or segments. Residual bitter taste is removed by boiling the albedo, the name given to the white spongy portion of the peel, for a period of half an hour in water. The boiled peels are then placed in running cold water overnight to remove any final traces of the bitter oils. The resulting peels will have at this stage a yellowish colour and a soft but firm texture free of bitter taste. The peels are then rolled into a cylindrical form and a thin thread passed across the centre of the cylinder. This thread helps to maintain the shape of the peels during the boiling step that follows. Boiling is carried out by adding the peels to a hot sugar syrup. The syrup is prepared by mixing sugar and water at the ratio of 2:1 (w/w). The weight of sugar is equal to the weight of the peels. The mixture is boiled, and the resulting broth is skimmed off the surface. The peels are added to this hot syrup, and boiling is continued until the peels become soft and translucent. Heating is then discontinued, and the peels are allowed to cool before removing and dipping in crystalline sugar. The sugar crystals adhere to the cooked peels, which are individually rearranged to the cylindrical form and preserved without refrigeration in covered boxes.

Nutritive value. Like all other jams and preserves, this food is particularly rich in food calories from its high sugar and carbohydrate content. In general the albedo is considered to be rich in cellulose, hemicellulose, lignin, pectic substances and phenolic compounds. All the water-soluble

TABLE 60
Proximate gross composition of fresh and dried lemons
(value per 100 g edible portion)

Component	Fresh lemon	Dried lemon
Energy value *(kcal)*	43	327
Moisture *(g)*	89.8	16.3
Protein *(g)*	0.7	7.8
Lipids *(g)*	0.6	2.7
Ash *(g)*	0.4	5.3
Crude fibre *(g)*	0.7	–
Carbohydrates *(g)*	7.8	67.6

vitamins and volatile oils originally present in the tissue are lost during the boiling and washing procedures.

Dried limes and lemons. Limes and lemons are grown in some parts of the Arabian Gulf, particularly in the Sultanate of Oman. Traditionally when lemons are in season, lemon drink (*sherbat al-loomi*) is commonly consumed. It is believed that lemon drink helps in curing nausea and vomiting. Lemon drink is prepared by squeezing the lemon in water and adding sugar as required.

When large quantities of lemon are available, the lemons are sundried and stored for future use. Dried lemons, called *loomi aswad* (black lemon) are used in most Gulf dishes to perfume and flavour them. Dried lemons are sometimes ground to a powder. This product has a long shelf-life because of its low moisture content.

Preparation. The dried lemons are prepared by boiling the fruits with water and salt for three to five minutes. The water is then drained, and the lemons are placed on a metal-mesh cake rack under direct sunlight for one week to dry. The lemons are ready for use when they become dark and the flesh completely dehydrated. The dried lemons can be stored in airtight containers for several months.

The composition of fresh and dried lemons is illustrated in Table 60.

Jujube

Jujube *(Ziziphus spina-christi)*, known as *kinar* or *nabk* in Oman and Saudi Arabia, is grown throughout all Arabian Gulf countries. The fruits, which are commonly consumed fresh, are ovoid, 2-3 cm long, with fleshy, acid pulp and a hard stone. The tree is known as *cidar* or *cidrah*, and its leaves are widely used in folk medicine. In general the jujube tree can survive under very unfavourable conditions of soil, water and weather.

Commercially, the fruits can be utilized in different ways. They can be used to prepare a refreshing drink or sundried and stored for a long period of time. It was found that after drying for a few weeks, the fruits acquire a soft and appealing texture similar to that of dates. The dried kinars can be used like raisins in cooked rice or utilized in the making of chutney and pickles. Kinars are very popular and are sold in the local market when in season.

Nutritive value. The fruit in general is rich in protein, vitamin C and some minerals, compared with other fruits. Data on the amino-acid content of kinar at the ripe stage shows a very high level of threonine and a complete absence of methionine. For its composition, see Table 61.

Doum

Doum refers to the fruit of the doum palm (*Hyphaene thebaica* Mart.) which has been known since the time of ancient Egyptians. Doum palm is found throughout the Sudan and to a lesser extent in Upper Egypt. The fruit is similar to plums, of about 7-8 cm in diameter, with one central stone and a spongy, sugary pericarp (pulp) of characteristic agreeable taste. The pericarp is the only portion used as a food and is very popular among children. At the household level, the pericarp is steeped in water, and the water extract is used as a popular drink. Utilization of doum fruits at the industrial level is limited to button-making from the stones and animal feed from its by-products.

TABLE 61
Proximate gross composition and mineral content of jujube
(value per 100 g edible portion)

Component	Value
Energy value *(kcal)*	90
Moisture *(g)*	77.2
Protein *(g)*	1.6
Lipids *(g)*	0.3
Ash *(g)*	0.6
Crude fibre *(g)*	–
Carbohydrates *(g)*	20.4
Calcium (mg)	43
Phosphorus *(mg)*	28
Iron *(mg)*	0.9
Sodium *(mg)*	6
Zinc *(mg)*	–

Preparation. For domestic preparation of doum drink, the pericarp is separated and steeped in water overnight, the extract is then strained through muslin cloth, boiled and sweetened with sugar to taste and served as a cold summer drink. It has a pleasant characteristic taste and dark yellowish colour. Experimental research has been carried out, aimed at the preparation of a concentrate from doum extract to be utilized in bottled soft drinks and carbonated beverages.

The nutritive value of doum is shown in Table 62.

VEGETABLES
Baba ghannouj
Baba ghannouj is a tehineh-based dip (see p. 146) that has eggplant as the main ingredient. It is a popular food mostly consumed as a dip or a side dish with an oil dressing and is available in the markets of Lebanon, Jordan, the Syrian Arab Republic and Iraq as a canned food.

TABLE 62
Proximate gross composition and nutritive value of *doum*
(value per 100 g, dry-weight basis)

Component	Value
Energy value *(kcal)*	268
Moisture *(g)*	10.6
Total soluble solids *(g)*	70.4
Protein *(g)*	3.2
Ether extract *(g)*	1.4
Reducing sugars *(g)*	14.1
Glucose *(g)*	9.3
Fructose *(g)*	4.7
Sucrose *(g)*	37.4
Acid hydrolysable polysaccharides *(g)*	9.1
Cellulose and hemicellulose *(g)*	23.5
Crude fibres *(g)*	12.2
Ash *(g)*	8
Total acidity (as citric acid) *(g)*	1.5

Preparation. Eggplants are usually broiled on low fire with frequent turning to ensure homogeneous exposure to heat. Usually varieties of eggplants that bear round fruits are preferred. The skins of the eggplants are removed after broiling with the aid of a strong jet of cold water. The remaining pulp is then mashed in a mill or blender with frequent addition of tehineh. The amount of tehineh added is around 15 percent of the weight of the fresh eggplant, and an equal volume of lemon juice (or diluted solution of citric acid) is also added. The final mix is brought to 1.5 percent of sodium chloride and then packed in cans. For immediate home consumption, ground garlic is also added, but in canned products, garlic is added by the consumer.

Nutritive value. Since baba ghannouj is a vegetable-based food, it is a rather dilute source of nutrients. Its relatively high energy content is contributed by the tehineh component.
Its composition per 100 g edible portion is as follows:
- Energy value *(kcal)*   106
- Moisture   78
- Protein   3.5
- Lipids   3.7
- Carbohydrates   12.6

Brined grape leaves

Grape leaves are commonly consumed fresh with certain salads or used in some cooked dishes to wrap rice stuffings, which may or may not include meat. However, since fresh grape leaves are abundant in the early part of the growing season, when vines are partially defoliated to expose the grape clusters to sunshine, such leaves are usually pickled in glass jars and stored for later use during the winter season.

Preparation. Grape leaves contain a natural mould inhibitor that facilitates their preservation tremendously. Since the leaves are thin and delicate and must remain as intact as possible to be used, the presence of the naturally occurring preservative comes as a great advantage, since it eliminates the need of any harsh treatment during their preservation. The brine is usually prepared by the egg flotation method, where enough sodium chloride (table salt) is dissolved in the water so that an egg floats when placed in the brine. Such a brine usually contains 12 percent salt (w/v). The washed and dried leaves are then packed individually one on top of the other in a glass jar. Care should be taken to arrange the leaves as flatly and as uniformly as possible without wrinkling or damaging the leaf tissue. Hot brine is then poured on the stocked leaves, until they are well covered with the liquid. The jars are closed while hot and allowed to cool before storage.

Nutritive value. Grape leaves are mainly used for their special sour taste and their ability to be conveniently wrapped to contain certain stuffings. They

TABLE 63
Proximate gross composition of brined grape leaves
(value per 100 g edible portion)

Component	Value
Energy value *(kcal)*	97
Moisture *(g)*	75
Protein *(g)*	3.8
Lipids *(g)*	1
Ash *(g)*	1.5
Crude fibre *(g)*	2.6
Nitrogen-free extract *(g)*	15.6

serve as a good source of organic acids and, when fresh, may act as a source of vitamins. They are considered to be of poor nutritive value (see Table 63).

Dried okra
Okra pods (*Hibiscus esculentus*) lend themselves to dehydration better than any other green vegetable. They retain their colour and shape and have the ability to rehydrate quite readily when placed in water.

Preparation. Fresh, tender okra pods are preferred. They should be free of diseases, insect damage or other contaminants. With the help of a needle and a long string, each pod is individually tied by passing the needle and string through its basal part near the pedicel. The result is a long string with okra pods hanging uniformly along its length. This method gives the vegetable an ample chance to be exposed to the air all the time. If dehydration is carried out in the shade, the resulting colour of the dried pods will be greener and more desirable than if dehydration is carried out in the sun. Okra pods are always covered with fine short hairs that collect dust, dirt and insect eggs. If proper hot-air dehydration is carried out, followed by aseptic packaging, a better quality product can be expected.

TABLE 64
Proximate gross composition of dried okra
(value per 100 g edible portion)

Component	Value
Energy value *(kcal)*	49
Moisture *(g)*	87
Protein *(g)*	2.2
Lipids *(g)*	0.2
Ash *(g)*	0.8
Crude fibre *(g)*	1
Carbohydrates *(g)*	8.7

Nutritive value. Okra has a characteristic mucilage component, probably of carbohydrate origin, that gives it special appeal to some people. Table 64 illustrates its composition.

Crushed green olives

Preservation of olives is part of the traditions of all the countries of the Near East, and all the processing methods rely on soaking the olives in brine to develop their taste. No lye treatment is followed to any extent to remove the bitter compounds. Basically processed olives are of two kinds, depending on their skin colour: green olives or black olives. The change in colour is due to the stage of maturity at which the fruits are picked, green olives being most common and the crushed type the most popular.

Preparation. Traditionally, the olives used to be cracked individually by hitting them with a mallet or stone, taking care not to break the seeds. In recent times, sorting machines that separate the fruits according to their size allow the use of cracking machines that can do the job very efficiently and at tremendous speed. The cracked olives are then soaked in water for three days with daily removal and changing of the water. At the end of this period,

TABLE 65
Proximate gross composition of green olives
(value per 100 g edible portion)

Component	Value
Energy value *(kcal)*	132
Moisture *(g)*	75.2
Protein *(g)*	1.5
Lipids *(crude ether extract)* *(g)*	13.5
Ash *(g)*	5.8
Crude fibre *(g)*	1.2

the olives are well drained and packed in sterilized glass pod jars and covered with brine containing slices of lemon and some hot pepper. The concentration of salt in the brine is controlled by the egg-flotation method (12 percent w/v of sodium chloride), and the use of twist-off caps ensures absence of contamination. The olives are usually marketed three weeks after processing.

The composition of green olives can be seen in Table 65.

Harissa or hrouss

Harissa, or chilli paste, is a typical and largely consumed traditional food in Tunisia. There are few foods in the Tunisian national diet that do not include harissa at any stage during their preparation. The chilli paste with its typical dark-red colour is the most common condiment. With the many spices added to it during its preparation (coriander, caraway, salt, garlic, etc.), harissa becomes an indispensable ingredient. Harissa is also consumed on its own, spread on a piece of bread to relieve an irresistible hunger.

Preparation. Two types of harissa are available; one is made from dry pepper and the other from fresh red pepper. In the first preparation, dried red peppers are cleaned and their seeds removed before steeping them in warm

TABLE 66
Proximate gross composition of *harissa*
(value per 100 g edible portion)

Component	Value
Energy value *(kcal)*	35
Moisture *(g)*	87.7
Protein *(g)*	0.4
Lipids *(g)*	0.3
Ash *(g)*	0.7
Crude fibre *(g)*	2
Carbohydrates *(g)*	8.9

water for one to two hours. They are then mashed with garlic, salt, caraway and coriander seeds. The final product obtained, in the form of a smooth paste, is stored in glass or earthenware jars and covered with olive oil. The addition of olive oil protects against contact with air and improves the keeping quality of the product.

The second type of harissa is processed exactly in the same way, except that fresh red peppers are used instead of dried peppers. Addition of spices in the right proportions is critical to both taste and preservation of the final product. Both types of harissa are produced and canned on a large scale.

See Table 66 for an analysis of the composition of harissa.

Felfel zina or *felfla*

Felfel zina (chilli powder) is a common ingredient used frequently in the preparation of stews and sauces. It is made of ground red peppers after maturation. Felfel zina is produced in Tunisia in two main varieties: hot pepper, which gives felfel zina har (hot), and sweet pepper, which gives felfel zina hlou (sweet).

TABLE 67
Proximate gross composition of *felfel zina*
(value per 100 g edible portion)

Component	Value
Energy value *(kcal)*	269
Moisture *(g)*	12.9
Protein *(g)*	20.2
Lipids *(g)*	14.2
Ash *(g)*	6.4
Crude fibre *(g)*	22.9
Carbohydrates *(g)*	15.3

Preparation. Pepper pods are harvested when they reach maturity and turn red. They are then allowed to wilt by exposing them to the air for a period of two to three days. They are then strung on long strings and suspended on horizontal ropes, until they are completely dry. After dehydration, the peppers are subjected to a grinding and sieving operation, either alone or with caraway, coriander seeds, salt and dry, crushed garlic. The ground product is sieved to separate the outer skins and the coarse particles, and the powder is retained and stored in large containers or in linen sacks.

Felfel zina is produced on a family-cottage scale and marketed through commercial outlets and street vendors. Packaging of chilli powder, alone or combined with other spices, is also possible. There is, however, large scope for improving the preparation, grading and packaging of this ingredient.

Table 67 illustrates the composition of felfel zina.

Slata meshwiya

In the summer months, when seasonal peppers and tomatoes are abundant, vegetables are usually roasted or broiled and heavily spiced to make *slata meshwiya*, served as an entry to many dishes. In many areas, however,

TABLE 68
Proximate gross composition of *slata meshwiya*
(value per 100 g edible portion)

Component	Value
Energy value *(kcal)*	135
Moisture *(g)*	70.1
Protein *(g)*	2.7
Lipids *(crude ether extract) (g)*	10.2
Carbohydrate *(g)*	13

meshwiya is eaten with bread, and it constitutes the whole meal. Meshwiya is also served as a dressing for fish dishes in seafood restaurants.

Preparation. Peppers, red and green tomatoes and onions are broiled over a charcoal fire until they are well cooked. The vegetables are then peeled and cut into fine pieces or ground and seasoned with preserved capers, salt, ground caraway, coriander seeds and sprinkled with olive oil.

Slata meshwiya is produced and canned on a large scale in Tunisia.

The data in Table 68 show the composition of slata meshwiya.

Dukkous

Dukkous is a flavouring that is commonly used in the Arabian Gulf area and is usually served with rice. It is a sauce prepared from tomatoes, garlic, chilli, salt and oil. Dukkous is prepared at home or produced commercially as a pasteurized product. Pasteurized dukkous can be stored at room temperature with a shelf-life of six months.

Preparation. For preparation, tomatoes are sliced and mixed with oil, ground garlic and salt. The mixture is then simmered over low heat until well cooked. Chillies are added at the end of the cooking stage and mixed well.

TABLE 69
Proximate gross composition and mineral content of *dukkous*
(value per 100 g edible portion)

Component	Value
Energy value *(kcal)*	81
Moisture *(g)*	80.5
Protein *(g)*	2.2
Lipids *(g)*	4.8
Ash *(g)*	5.2
Crude fibre *(g)*	-
Carbohydrates *(g)*	7.3
Calcium *(mg)*	58
Phosphorus *(mg)*	63
Iron *(mg)*	0.94
Sodium *(mg)*	–
Zinc *(mg)*	0.49

Dukkous is eaten in small quantities as chutney; therefore, its contribution to the daily nutrient intake is insignificant.
See Table 69 for an analysis of the composition of dukkous.

Bibliography

Al-Mohizea, I.S., El-Behery, M.M. & Havlass, M.A. 1986. Chemical characteristics of jujube fruits grown in the Central Region of Saudi Arabia. *J. Coll. Agric. King Saud Univ.*, 8: 337-344.

FAO. 1988. *Traditional food plants*, FAO Food and Nutrition Paper No. 42, p. 531-537.

Hubert, A. 1984. *Le pain et l'olive: aspects de l'alimentation en Tunisie.* Centre régional de publication. Lyons, Editions du CNRS.

INS. 1975. *Table de composition des aliments tunisiens.* Institut national de la statistique. Claude Jardin, FAO Consultant, Tunis.

Kamel, B.S. & Allam, M. 1979. *Composition of foods consumed in Kuwait (Phase I)*, p. 19. Kuwait Institute for Scientific Research.

Khatchadourian, H.A., Sawaya, W.N., Khalil, J.K., Safi, W.M. & Mashadi, A.A. 1982. Utilization of dates *(Phoenix dactylifera* L.) grown in the Kingdom of Saudi Arabia in various date products. In *Proc. First Symposium on the Date Palm*, p. 504-518. Saudi Arabia, King Faisal University.

Mallos, T. 1983. *The complete Middle East cookbook*, p. 245. Sydney, Lansdowne Press.

Miller, A.G. & Morris, M. 1988. *Plants of Dhofar*, p. 246-247. The Office of the Advice for Conservation of the Environment. Diwan of Royal Court, Sultanate of Oman.

Passat, F.F. 1971. *The industrialization of date palm products*, p. 120. Baghdad, Al-Adib Printing Press. (in Arabic)

Pellett, P.L. & Shadarevian, S. 1970. *Food composition tables for use in the Middle East*, p. 18. Beirut, Lebanon, American University of Beirut Press.

Sawaya, W.N. 1986. Dates of Saudi Arabia. In Hamda, I.Y., El-Nawawy, A. & Mameesh, M., eds. *Advances in food industries development in the Arab world*, p. 109-136. Kuwait, Kuwait Institute for Scientific Research.

Sawaya, W.N., Khalil, J.K., Khatchadourian, H.A., Safi, W.M. & Mashadi, A.S. 1982. Sugars, tannins, and some vitamin contents of twenty-five date cultivars grown in Saudi Arabia at the Kahlal (mature colour) and Tamer (ripe) stage. In *Proc. First Symposium on the Date Palm*, p. 468-478. Saudi Arabia, King Faisal University.

Sawaya, W.N., Khalil, J.K., Safi, W.M.J. & Al-Shalfat, A. 1983. Physical and chemical characterization of three Saudi date cultivars at various stages of development. *Can. Inst. Food Sci. Technol. J.*, 16: 87-91.

Chapter 5
Beverages, sweets and confection

BEVERAGES
Licorice extract

Licorice refers to the roots of the plant *Glycyrrhiza glabra* L., which is grown between 30-45° northern latitude in Egypt, Iraq, Iran and China. Its national name in these countries refers to the edible part, the roots. It is named in Egypt and the Arab countries by the Arabic complex term *erq sus*, meaning sweet root. It is known in Italy by *dolce radice*, meaning sweet roots, and in Germany by *Suesholz*, meaning sweet wood.

The plant is propagated by rhizome division, and the yield may reach 20 tonnes per 0.5 hectares. Licorice was known to the ancient Egyptians for its medicinal benefits as well as its benefit as a thirst quencher. Nowadays, it is used extensively for the preparation of a popular summer drink. The drink is prepared at home and by shops that serve soft drinks.

Preparation. Licorice roots are usually skinned, cut and milled to shreds. The shredded roots are sometimes sold as such in retail. For the preparation of the extract (the drink), the shredded roots are rubbed manually with water and left for a few hours at room temperature. The mash is then transferred to a funnel containing palm-tree fibres, which serve as a filter. The mash is allowed to drip under tap water into a container underneath the funnel. The resulting extract is then diluted to the desired taste and colour. It may also be drum dried. Sodium bicarbonate may be added to the extract to give it a darker colour and a sweeter taste.

The industrial extraction of the shredded roots is carried out in special equipment under low vapour pressure, then concentrated under vacuum to about 18° Brix syrup (1.142 g/cc density). The extract may be further

TABLE 70
Proximate gross composition and nutritive value of licorice
(value per 100 g, dry-weight basis)

Component	Value
Energy value *(kcal)*	184
Moisture *(g)*	11.9
Total soluble solids *(g)*	34.2
Protein *(g)*	6.7
Lipids *(ether extract) (g)*	5.1
Reducing sugars *(g)*	1.4
Sucrose *(g)*	0.0045
Starch *(g)*	25.1
Cellulose and hemicellulose *(g)*	24.9
Crude fibres *(g)*	22.4
Ash *(g)*	8.2
Acidity (as citric acid) *(g)*	1.2
Glycyrrhizic acid *(g)*	8.4

concentrated to a dark-brown paste of 18-25 percent moisture content, drawn while hot, cooled, cut into pieces and stacked into cases lined with waterproof paper.

Nutritive value. Licorice contains traces of non-reducing sugars and a small amount of little-reducing sugars. The immense sweetness of licorice extract is due to its glycyrrhizic-acid content. It is 50 times sweeter than sucrose and can easily be diluted in a solution with a concentration as low as 1/20 000, forming the sweetest natural material known.

Licorice extract is consumed in Egypt as a popular thirst quencher of little caloric value and many medicinal benefits. Licorice is reported to possess diuretic, demulcent, and adrenal-hormone-like properties and a curative quality for certain gastric and stomach ulcers. Table 70 illustrates its composition.

Karkade

Roselle (known in Arabic as *karkade*) refers to the calyces of the fruit of the roselle plant (*Hibiscus sabdariffa* L.); an annual and sometimes perennial bush about 1.5-2 m high, cultivated in the Sudan, Upper Egypt, and in general throughout the tropics and subtropics. After the fruits are gathered, the calyces, which have a deep red or pink colour, are separated and dried. The yield per 0.5 ha can reach 250 kg. Dried calyces are used in Egypt and the Sudan in the preparation of a traditional, acidic, refreshing beverage served cold or hot as a substitute for tea in summer and winter. Calyces are also ground and packed in small bags of high porosity, each containing 2 g ground calyces to be used directly for preparing the hot beverage in winter, as is the case with tea bags. In the Sudan, calyces are water extracted and drum- or spray-dried, and the powder is sold in closed containers weighing 100 g each.

Preparation. For the preparation of karkade drink, at homes and at shops serving soft drinks, the calyces are steeped in water for about one hour, after which the suspension is passed through a tea sieve or muslin cloth. The residue may be re-extracted, and the clear filtrates are combined together, sweetened to taste and cooled in a refrigerator. Hot drinks are usually extracted in hot water, as is the case with tea leaves.

In the Sudan, where the crop is abundant, the water extract is concentrated, then drum-dried to a powder and packed in small containers. The powder is readily soluble in cold and hot water and is consumed after sweetening with sugar. The resulting beverage has a pleasant acidic taste and a characteristic flavour.

Nutritive value. Roselle is characterized by high acidity (mainly tartaric and malic acids) and low total-sugar content, with a low caloric value (see Table 71).

TABLE 71
Proximate gross composition and nutritive value of *karkade*
(value per 100 g, dry-weight basis)

Component	Value
Energy value *(kcal)*	153
Moisture *(g)*	13.9
Total soluble solids *(g)*	62.6
Protein *(g)*	8.2
Ether extract *(g)*	8.6
Reducing sugars *(g)*	3.3
Glucose *(g)*	1.1
Fructose *(g)*	2.1
Sucrose *(g)*	0.069
Acid hydrolysable polysaccharides *(g)*	7.2
Total acidity (as citric acid) *(g)*	20.8
Cellulose and hemicellulose *(g)*	20.9
Crude fibres *(g)*	9.5
Ash *(g)*	8.7

Roselle extract, traditionally known as karkade drink, is consumed in the Sudan and Egypt as a popular thirst quencher in summer and as a substitute for tea in winter. It is preferred to other soft drinks because of its well-known medicinal virtues, such as reduction of blood pressure, stimulation of intestinal peristalsis and diuretic effect.

Qahwah

Qahwah is light coffee consumed very frequently by the people in the Gulf countries. It can be prepared in various ways, but always without sugar. It is a traditional welcoming drink served at all social occasions. It is served from a traditional pot *dallah* into a very small cup without handles *finjan*, in small quantities of about 25 ml each.

Preparation. Qahwah is prepared from water, coffee, cardamom, saffron and rose water. The coffee beans are roasted in a large, shallow frying pan over medium heat until they turn golden brown. The coffee beans are then slightly cooled and ground coarsely in a coffee grinder *(hawan)*; nowadays an electic grinder is used. Water is then added to the ground coffee and brought to a boil. Cardamom, rose water and saffron are then added to the boiling water. After a few minutes of boiling, the solution is poured into a dallah, while the ground coffee residue is retained in the saucepan.

Nutritive value. Qahwah has no significant nutritional value, because it is a very light coffee and contains no sugar. The coffee is sometimes recommended for obese people to be taken before a meal to decrease their appetite for food.

Tamr hindi

Tamarind *(tamr hindi* in Arabic) refers to the fleshy part of the pods of the plant *Tamarindus indica* L. Tamarind is well-known in Egypt, the Sudan and many of the Arab countries as the basis of a popular, slightly acidic summer drink.

Preparation. Tamarind is sold in the market as dried, deshelled pods that are seed-free. For the preparation of tamarind drink, the flesh is soaked in water for at least two hours, and preferably overnight. The mixture is then brought to boiling and held at boiling temperature for a few minutes. It is then cooled to room temperature and strained in muslin cloth. The residue may be re-extracted and the filtrates combined together, diluted and sweetened to taste. The drink is usually served as such in drinking glasses in homes and at shops serving soft drinks. Experimental research has been carried out for bottling and concentration of tamarind extract.

Nutritive value. Tamarind is characterized by its high acidity, high content of reducing sugars and the absence of sucrose (see Table 72). It contains also polysaccharides (about 4.57 percent) other than starch, which are hydrolysable by acid to reducing sugars. Sweetening tamarind extract by

TABLE 72
Proximate gross composition and nutritive value of *tamr hindi* (value per 100 g, dry-weight basis)

Component	Value
Energy value *(kcal)*	249
Moisture *(g)*	25.5
Total soluble solids *(g)*	76.6
Protein *(g)*	3.6
Ether extract *(g)*	3.9
Reducing sugars *(g)*	43.8
Glucose *(g)*	18.6
Fructose *(g)*	25.2
Non-reducing sugars *(g)*	-
Acidity (as tartaric acid) *(g)*	15.4
Acid hydrolysable polysaccharides *(g)*	21
Crude fibres *(g)*	8.9
Ash *(g)*	9.3

sugar raises its caloric value, which together with its natural acidity, gives it a pleasant and appealing taste.

Hulu mur

This soft drink is prepared from fermented flour of *Sorghum bicolor*. It is red and has a sweet-sour taste. It is widely consumed in the Sudan, especially during the month of Ramadan.

Preparation. The first stage is to prepare malted sorghum grains by soaking the grains overnight, then spreading them on cloth sheets in layers less than 2 cm thick. The seeds are kept moist by frequent sprinkling with water, until germination is completed in about two days. At the end of this period, the shoots reach 1-3 cm in length, and water application is withheld from the seeds for one day. During this final day, the seeds develop a reddish colour and are removed to dry out in the sun. The sundried malt is then ground into fine flour and can be used to produce *hulu mur*.

Unmalted sorghum grains are ground with flour and mixed with water to form a soft dough. The proportion of flour to water is usually 2:3 (w/v). The dough is then half-baked on a hot steel plate and mixed again with half its weight of sorghum malt flour. More water is added, and a starter prepared from fermented kisra bread (see p. 10) is used to initiate the fermentation. The dough is left to ferment for 12 hours, after which the following spices are added: coriander, cardamom, black cumin, cinnamon, *khurunjal*, fenugreek, black cumin, karkade and ginger. Dates and tamarind are also added to the dough in the form of a seed-free thick paste. More water may be added before mixing the dough again and allowing it a final fermentation period of 18 hours. The fermented dough mass is then divided into pieces, rolled into thin sheets and baked on a hot steel plate. The baked sheets can be stored for some time or soaked directly in water to yield hulu-mur drink. The drink is usually sweetened with sugar before consumption.

SWEETS AND CONFECTION
Halwa

Halwa is one of the most frequently consumed traditional sweets in the Gulf. It is usually eaten before drinking coffee, and it is the main sweet served to visitors. Halwa is prepared from corn (maize) starch, water, fat, sugar, nuts, cardamom, and saffron.

Preparation. Corn (maize) flour is mixed with water and put over a low fire. Sugar, nuts, cardamom and saffron are then added, and the mixture is stirred constantly. Fat (butter or samin) is gradually added and stirring continued until a thick paste is formed. The paste (halwa) is put in small containers and kept at room temperature for further use.

Nutritive value. From the nutritional point of view, the high content of animal fat in halwa makes this sweet high in calories and saturated fatty acids. Halwa is low in protein and minerals (see Table 73).

TABLE 73
Proximate gross composition of *halwa*
(value per 100 g edible portion)

Component	Value
Energy value *(kcal)*	393
Moisture *(g)*	15.3
Protein *(g)*	1
Lipids *(g)*	11.4
Ash *(g)*	0.2
Crude fibre *(g)*	0.6
Carbohydrates *(g)*	71.5

Nashab

Nashab, also called *darabeel* in Kuwait, is a traditional food that is widely consumed at weddings and other social occasions. It is mostly served with Arabic coffee. Nashab is produced commercially in Bahrain and Kuwait. This food can be stored for a long time, mainly because of its very low moisture content.

Preparation. The major ingredients used in the preparation of nashab are: wheat flour, sugar, ground almonds, cardamom powder, rose water and oil. A soft dough is prepared from water and wheat flour and spread into a thin sheet. Rectangular pieces (10 x 25 cm) are cut from the dough sheets and brushed with oil. The sugar, cardamom, ground almonds and rose water are mixed until a crumbly mixture is formed. The mixture is then stuffed in the dough rectangles and rolled. The rolled, stuffed pastries are fried in oil until brown and then strained.

TABLE 74
Proximate gross composition of *nashab*
(value per 100 g edible portion)

Component	Value
Energy value *(kcal)*	423
Moisture *(g)*	4.2
Protein *(g)*	8.5
Lipids *(g)*	9.6
Ash *(g)*	1
Crude fibre *(g)*	1.1
Carbohydrates *(g)*	75.7

The composition of nashab is shown in Table 74.

Halawa tehineyah

Halawa tehineyah is a product made of tehineh, sucrose, glucose, citric acid and a small amount of saponin, an extract prepared from the roots and bark of the tree *Saponaria officinalis*. It is known as *rahash* in the Gulf and *halwa shamiyah* in the Maghreb countries.

Halawa tehineyah is a popular sweet food consumed in all the countries of the Near East. It was introduced to the region by emigrant Turks over 100 years ago and was known at that time as *asmierly halawa*; it was then processed locally and known as halawa tehineyah or halawa shamiyah.

Preparation. Halawa tehineyah is processed by dissolving sugar in water (3:1, w/w); no water is added if commercial glucose is used. The sugar solution is then heated to 149°C in steam-jacketed cookers, fitted with strong rotating paddles for mixing the sugar solution. Citric acid is then added, if sucrose is used, at a ratio of 1 g:1 000 g sucrose), and heating continues for 60-70 minutes. Cooking is considered to be complete when the sugar can be transformed into solid threads after cooling. Prior to complete cooking, an emulsifying agent is added to the semi-solid sugar mass with vigorous mixing. Heating is then stopped, but mixing continues for an additional five to ten minutes, if commercial glucose is used, or ten to 20 minutes, if sucrose is used. This step incorporates air into the mixture and renders it a light and shiny white mass. This cooked mass is then poured, while hot, into an equal amount of tehineh by weight, some vanilla extract is added, and the mixture is manipulated by hand to the right consistency. The mixture is then distributed in tin frames, left to cool at room temperature, then wrapped in waxed paper and/or aluminium foil, then packed in appropriate plastic or tin containers.

An extract of saponaria root or bark is usually used as an emulsifying and plasticizing agent. It is added to the mixture prior to the end of the cooking process. Saponaria extract is prepared by boiling about 5 kg of ground bark in about 6-8 litres of water and leaving it to steep for three days, during which about 6 litres of water are added consecutively. The resulting volume of extract reaches then about 16 litres, 1 litre of which is usually added to 110 kg of sugar utilized for halawa processing.

Saponaria extract gives the final product a light colour and a fluffy texture and decreases the tendency of its oil to separate during storage. The active component is its content of saponins (glycosides of hemolytic activity). Saponaria extract is not permitted to be added to foods, except in the manufacture of halawa tehineyah, since residual saponin is very low. Experimental research has proven that other non-toxic emulsifying agents could be successfully used, however they are not applied by the industry as yet.

Nutritive value. Halawa tehineyah has a high nutritive value, in addition to its pleasant taste. It is rich in oil and sugar and has a reasonably high protein content. Some manufacturers also incorporate nuts and/or dried fruits in special fancy brands, which increase its acceptability and nutritive value. In addition its protein contains reasonable amounts of essential amino-acids (see Table 75).

TABLE 75
Proximate gross composition and nutritive value of *halawa tehineyah*
(value per 100 g edible portion)

Component	25% sucrose	100% sucrose	100% sucrose, stuffed
Energy value *(kcal)*	519.8	522.8	512.8
Moisture *(g)*	3.5	3.1	2.9
Protein *(g)*	15.2	14.4	12.2
Ether extract *(g)*	29.1	29.2	26.2
Carbohydrates *(g)*	49.1	50.6	55.7
Crude fibre *(g)*	1.1	1.1	0.9
Total ash *(g)*	1.9	1.5	1.5
Calcium *(mg)*	90.9	73	70
Phosphorus *(mg)*	1186	1005	1167
Iron *(mg)*	166	173	136
Thiamine *(mg)*	0.15	173	136
Riboflavin *(mg)*	0.09	-	-
Niacin *(mg)*	3.0	-	-

Hommosiyah, semsamiyah and *fouliyah*

These three types of food are typical of pulled hard candy, coated with either chickpeas *(Cicer arientinum)*, sesame seeds *(Sasamum indicum)* or peanuts (Arachis hypogoia) to produce a type of candy named after these seeds, i.e. *hommosiyah, semsamiyah* or *fouliyah* respectively. These foods are traditional to Egypt, the Sudan and many of the Arab countries. In fact the word candy, meaning confection, is a term derived from the Arabic word *quandi*, meaning sugar.

This traditional type of hard candy is manufactured in large quantities by numerous factories of small capacity. It is very popular and extensively consumed, especially by children and school pupils, and serves as a high-calorie snack food during the day. Despite its wide consumption, no standards for identity and quality are set for this type of candy as yet. Products of different factories differ in composition and overall quality.

Preparation. The ingredients used in the manufacture of this type of traditional hard candy are cane sugar (40-75 percent) and commercial glucose (45Brix, 55-60 percent). The ratio of sucrose and commercial glucose that gives the best-quality candy mass is 75:25 respectively. The mixture is first cooked to produce the candy mass. Flavouring material (usually rose or banana flavour) is then added, followed by one of the coating seeds, usually 25-30 percent for chickpeas, 10-13 percent for sesame seeds and 30-35 percent for shelled and roasted peanuts or hazelnuts.

For the manufacture of the traditional, seed-coated hard candy, cane sugar is dissolved in one-third of its weight in water into a pan placed over an open fire or steam-jacketed kettle. A syrup of about 68° Brix is made and allowed to boil for about ten minutes. A quantity of commercial glucose, weighing about three-quarters of the weight of the initial quantity of cane sugar, is then added, and the mixture is further cooked with continuous agitation for about 30-40 minutes until the soft-crack stage is reached (about 143°C). Soft-crack stage is the stage at which the syrup, when dropped into very cold water, separates into threads that are hard and brittle.

Commercial glucose or corn (maize) syrup used in this type of hard candy is usually of the low-conversion type, containing about 31-40 percent reducing sugars and not more than 450 p.p.m. SO_2. The amount of reducing sugars in commercial glucose plays an important role in candy manufacture, since proper proportion of reducing sugars in the candy mass prevents stickiness and crumbling in the product.

The sugar mass is then poured over an oiled marble slab (paraffin oil or sesame-seed butter help keep the candy mass from sticking to the marble slab) and flavouring material is then added and mixed. The mass is then tempered to lower its temperature to about 70-80°C so that it acquires a plastic consistency and can be pulled manually or mechanically to incorporate air.

Pulling the candy mass is carried out manually in most factories by hanging the candy mass on a large iron nail fixed on the wall. The candy is pulled by hand, and the pulled end is then fixed again on the nail. This process is repeated for about 15 minutes till the mass has become milky white in colour. In modern factories, a pulling machine is utilized for this process. It is driven by a strong motor and consists of three steel arms, two of which rotate in opposite directions; the third, which is stationary, is placed in between. The mass is worked by this machine for about seven to ten minutes.

The pulled candy mass is then returned to the oiled marble slab and kneaded manually to acquire a uniform appearance before transferring it to a heated steel slab and rolling it manually to a cylindrical shape of about 5-7 cm in diameter. It is then cut into pieces of about 20 cm in length.

In the meantime, cleaned and dehulled seeds (sesame seeds are not dehulled) are partially roasted to facilitate their adhesion to the candy rolls. The partially roasted seeds are then spread in thin layers over the slab, and the pulled candy is rolled over and pressed to push the seeds into the pulled candy. The process may be carried out by means of wooden cylinders that flatten the pieces of candy and press them into the roasted seeds spread on the slab.

The candy mass is then flattened to the desired thickness and cut into pieces by a special forming and cutting machine. Candy pieces are then stowed on a cold marble slab to cool and acquire a final desirable hardness. The cut pieces of candy are then wrapped in cellophane paper and properly packed.

Nutritive value. The nutritive value of seed-coated candy is dependent upon the type and amount of seeds used (see Table 76).

Seed-coated candy has a long shelf-life, if the commercial glucose used in its manufacture does not exceed 25 percent of the sugar mixture, and if the product is wrapped in sealed polyethylene films of 35-50 μ thickness. Using increased proportions of commercial glucose accelerates moisture absorption and hence quick deterioration in quality. Establishing standards for identity and quality of this type of candy would improve the quality, increase acceptability and facilitate marketing.

TABLE 76
Proximate gross composition and nutritive value of hard seed-coated candy (value per 100 g, dry-weight basis)

Component	Hommosiyah	Semsamiyah	Fouliyah
Energy value *(kcal)*	400	486	472
Moisture *(g)*	70	5.9	7.3
Protein *(g)*	9.9	2.4	12.3
Total lipids *(g)*	2.6	6.8	15.3
Total carbohydrates *(g)*	84.2	88.8	71.4
Reducing sugars *(g)*	13.6	16.4	14.2
Total ash *(g)*	1.7	1	1.3
Calcium *(mg)*	131	251	28.6
Iron *(mg)*	1.1	0.9	1
Phosphorus *(mg)*	210	134	169

Sambosa helwah

Sambosa helwah is a traditional sweet that is widely consumed in the Arabian Gulf countries, principally in Bahrain, Kuwait and Qatar. This sweet is served for visitors at weddings and at feasts. Traditionally sambosa helwah was prepared at home; recently, many local bakeries have developed commercial methods for preparing this sweet, and it is now available on the market in plastic bags weighing 1/2 or 1 kg.

Preparation. Wheat flour, sugar, ground almonds, cardamom powder, rose water, salt and saffron constitute the main ingredients of sambosa helwah.

For preparation, the almonds, sugar, cardamom, saffron and rose water are mixed well until a crumbly mixture is formed. The flour, oil, salt and water are kneaded until a soft dough is obtained. The dough is then formed into sheets, which are cut into strips (approximately 2 x 11 cm). The mixture is then placed on the dough sheets, which are folded into triangles. The edges

TABLE 77
Proximate gross composition of *sambosa helwah*
(value per 100 g edible portion)

Component	Value
Energy value *(kcal)*	413
Moisture *(g)*	10.5
Protein *(g)*	5.4
Lipids *(g)*	12
Ash *(g)*	0.6
Crude fibre *(g)*	0.7
Carbohydrates *(g)*	70.8

are closed using a wet fork. The sambosa is deep-fried in corn (maize) oil until brown. Although the final product can be kept for a long time without deterioration in quality, sambosa is always preferred when it is warm.

Table 77 illustrates the nutritive value of sambosa helwah.

Mesfuf, rfissa or seffa

When couscous, prepared in the same way described on p. 20, is sweetened with sugar, raisins and/or dates, it is then called mesfuf (rfissa in Tunisia and seffa in Morocco). This food is frequently consumed during the holy month of Ramadan as the last meal before fasting or as a breakfast or dessert at other times of the year.

Preparation. Preparation of the basic ingredient — couscous — follows the same rules described earlier. Coarse grains of semolina are sprinkled with water and rolled with fine semolina particles to form the typical couscous grains. The product is then steamed over boiling water and the process repeated a second time after adding raisins or dates. At serving time, couscous is buttered or boiled and sprinkled with fine sugar. For every

TABLE 78
Proximate gross composition of some kinds of sweet couscous
(value per 100 g edible portion)

	Energy value (kcal)	Moisture (g)	Protein (g)	Lipids (g)	Carbohydrates (g)
Mesfuf with raisins	320	29	5.6	7.1	58.4
Rfissa (*mesfuf* with dates)	306	29	5.4	4.5	61
Mesfuf with milk	207	55.2	4.7	5.7	34.4

100 g of semolina, 120 g of butter, 60 g of olive oil, 400 g of sugar and 500 g of raisins or dates are needed. Milk can also be added to mesfuf.

For a comparison of the nutritive value of various types of sweet couscous, see Table 78.

Droo or sohlob
This sorghum-based porridge is usually consumed hot at breakfast or chilled and served as a dessert after meals. It is popular in Tunisia.

Preparation. The basic preparation involves roasting 100 g of sesame seeds and pounding them with an equal volume of sugar. Then 250 g of sorghum flour is added with 1 000 g of fine sugar and 5 litres of water or milk. The mixture is cooked on a medium heat and is stirred until the gruel thickens. The food is then flavoured with rose water before serving.

When sorghum is prepared in combination with almonds and nuts, the process becomes complex and elaborate. First a sorghum dough is made with 250 g of sorghum flour and a little water. This dough is divided into small balls and allowed to rest for half an hour. The balls are then immersed in boiling water for 15 minutes, drained and mashed. This product is then diluted in 750 ml of water and filtered through a thin cloth. The filtrate is saved. Sesame seeds, almonds and nuts are roasted, mashed and then

TABLE 79
Proximate gross composition of *droo*
(value per 100 g edible portion)

Component	Value
Energy value *(kcal)*	195
Moisture *(g)*	63
Protein *(g)*	5.3
Lipids *(crude ether extract)* *(g)*	10
Carbohydrates *(g)*	21.7

diluted in water and filtered as for sorghum. The two filtrates are mixed and put on a low heat for cooking. As the preparation starts thickening, the boiled milk is poured with the roasted and ground sesame seeds, and the mixture is stirred. The paste is then flavoured with geranium or rose water and served.

See Table 79 for an analysis of the composition of *droo*.

Makrudh

This pastry made with dates is extremely common in Tunisia and is appreciated at all occasions. It is made of wheat semolina, which is filled with dates and fried in vegetable oil. *Makrudh* is very specific to the Maghreb area and is hardly known outside the region.

Preparation. Medium semolina is mixed with plenty of oil and melted fat, sprinkled with a little water and a pinch of ground turmeric and then kneaded to obtain a firm paste, which is allowed to rest for half an hour. Meanwhile, dates with their stones removed are sprinkled with oil, flavoured with cinnamon and well mixed. The next step consists of filling the dough pieces with dates and shaping them into 10 x 5 cm lozenges. The filled pieces are then deep-fat fried until they acquire a golden colour, after which they are

TABLE 80
Proximate gross composition of *makrudh*
(value per 100 g edible portion)

Component	Value
Energy value *(kcal)*	432
Moisture *(g)*	16.9
Protein *(g)*	6.9
Lipids *(crude ether extract) (g)*	21.3
Carbohydrates *(g)*	54.9

immersed in honey or sugar syrup. Both syrup and paste are flavoured with a wide range of flavours: powdered orange peels, rose water, geranium water, orange-blossom water, etc.

Because of its long and elaborate processing, makrudh is now rarely prepared at home. Many pastry and delicatessen shops have specialized in the production and marketing of makrudh.

Table 80 shows a breakdown of the composition of makrudh.

Baklawah

Baklawah is a typical Near Eastern sweet that comes in different forms and shapes. Recipes vary slightly, but the basic form includes a layer of dough, then a layer of filling followed by another layer of dough.

Preparation. The dough used in the preparation of baklawah has to be in the form of very thin sheets. It can be prepared by mixing the following ingredients:

White fine flour	100 g
Salt	0.5 g
Water	25-30 g
Oil	10 g

TABLE 81
Proximate gross composition of *baklawah*
(value per 100 g edible portion)

Component	Value
Energy value *(kcal)*	549
Moisture *(g)*	7.3
Protein *(g)*	8.1
Lipids *(g)*	32.2
Ash *(g)*	1.2
Crude fibre *(g)*	0.8
Nitrogen-free extract *(g)*	50.4

The mixture is well kneaded until the gluten network develops, and the dough becomes smooth and shiny. At this stage the dough is allowed a rest period of about one hour at room temperature before being rolled into flat sheets. Those sheets are further flattened to a very thin form by special extruder-type machines or by hand, using a dowel. The pastry is rolled on to the dowel, and wheat starch is used as dusting powder. Unrolling the pastry and repeating the process results in dough sheets that are paper thin and that can be stacked on top of each other with a thin film of ghee applied in between.

In one presentation, the butter- or ghee-smeared stacks are cut into squares 10 x 110 cm and stacked 10 layers thick. In each group a small amount of filling is placed in the centre and the corners of the pastry folded over in the form of a flower. The baklawah is then baked.

The filling is usually prepared by mixing ground pistachio nuts with castor sugar, walnuts, almonds, rose water and some kind of binder such as egg albumin.

Baking is carried out at a medium oven temperature of about 175°C, and the temperature is reduced during the finishing stage. When the pastries are out of the oven, they are sprayed with a cooled sugar syrup flavoured with orange-blossom water and rose water. The delicious pastry is neatly packed in cellophane-covered boxes for long periods without need of refrigeration.

Nutritive value. Baklawah is a very concentrated food, particularly rich in fats and carbohydrates. For its composition, see Table 81.

Halkoum

Halkoum is a firm, gel-like confection that is based on gelatinized starch, sweetened with sugar and flavoured with rose water and orange-blossom water. It is popular among young children and old people, because of its easy mastication and pleasant mouthfeel. This food, which originated in Turkey, is now widely consumed in the Syrian Arab Republic, Lebanon, Jordan and the neighbouring countries.

Preparation. Invert sugar is prepared by heating a sucrose solution in the presence of an acid. Citric acid or lemon juice are used as acidulants. Under these conditions, the sucrose is hydrolyzed to its component sugars, namely glucose and fructose. A suspension of corn (maize) flour in water (1:4 w/w) is heated, with continuous stirring, until the starch gelatinizes and acquires a pale golden colour. Cream of tartar at the rate of 3-4 percent is usually added to the corn-flour suspension prior to heating. Rose water or orange-blossom water is added to the hot slurry and well mixed. Sometimes nuts are also added before pouring the mix in an oiled metal pan and allowing it to set for 12 hours. When the gel solidifies, it is cut into small cubes of 4 cm each side and coated with a mixture of powdered sugar and corn (maize) flour (3:1 w/w). Sometimes a pink colouring is added along with vanilla flavour, or a green colour with mint flavour. The product stores well at room temperature for long periods of time.

Nutritive value. Carbohydrates, in the form of sugar and starch, make up the major ingredient of halkoum. This food, therefore, is considered to be an excellent source of quick energy but very poor in its content of essential nutrients.

TABLE 82
Proximate gross composition of *manna*
(value per 100 g edible portion)

Component	Value
Energy value *(kcal)*	387
Moisture *(g)*	3
Protein *(g)*	1.8
Lipids *(g)*	0.8
Ash *(g)*	1.3
Crude fibre *(g)*	0.3
Nitrogen-free extract *(g)*	93

Manna

This confection is primarily produced in Iraq. The main ingredient used in its preparation is an exudate of the tree *Frakinus ornus*. This tree grows mainly in northern Iraq, and its exudate is probably a result of insect-produced wounds. The exudate accumulates on the leaves of the tree and is collected when the leaves fall to the ground. The sugars are then extracted with boiling water and concentrated to a sticky mass until use.

Preparation. A foamy sugar solution is prepared by dissolving sugar in water and adding a small proportion of egg white to it. The mixture is beaten until it becomes thick and foamy. At this stage, the sticky mass of *manna* is resuspended in water and added to the foamy syrup. The mixture is heated with continuous stirring until it becomes viscous. More egg white is added, and the rate of heating is decreased. Pistachio nuts are added and mixed well into the viscous mass. The manna in then spread in a layer 3-4 cm thick in a tray that has been sprinkled with flour. The manna is then allowed to solidify into a firm gel, which is cut into pieces of desired shape and size and coated with a mixture of flour and ground sugar before wrapping individually in cellophane film.

Nutritive value. Because of its content of egg white and pistachio nuts, manna offers some nutritious elements besides its desirable taste and high caloric value (see Table 82).

OTHER FOOD PRODUCTS
Tehineh

Tehineh is prepared from sesame seeds *(Sesamum indicum)* that are ground after roasting, either at steam temperature (white tehineh) or at higher temperature (red tehineh) to give a thick oily mixture of finely disintegrated solid material (mainly proteins) suspended in liquid sesame oil.

Tehineh may be eaten directly, either as a breakfast food mixed with pure molasses or as a salad dressing spiced mainly with garlic and eaten especially with fish dishes. In industry, red tehineh is the starting material for the production of sesame oil, whereas white tehineh is the main ingredient for the manufacture of halawa tehineyah (see p. 133), a popular breakfast food in many countries of the Near East and Turkey.

Preparation. White tehineh is processed by sifting sesame seeds to separate foreign matters. The seeds are then steeped in fresh water for a period of 6-10 hours, depending on seed variety and prevailing temperature. The seeds are then dehulled by a special dehulling machine, consisting of a great cauldron fitted with a moving piston that, upon operation, causes the seeds to rub against the bottom of the cauldron and against each other, resulting in the separation of seed coatings. The dehulled seeds (kernels) are then separated from the hulls by pouring the mixture in a brine solution (14-18 percent salt); the kernels float on the surface, whereas the hulls sink to the bottom. The dehulled kernels are then washed several times with fresh water to remove the salt. Excess water may be removed by centrifugation. The seeds are then roasted for about 2 hours in steam-heated roasters of semi-cylindrical shape equipped with moving paddles that provide continuous agitation during roasting. The roasted kernels are then aerated and cooled to room temperature by spreading them on agitated wooden platforms. They are then sifted to remove burnt seeds and hulls that would darken the tehineh after grinding. The roasted seeds are then crushed

TABLE 83
Mean composition and nutritive value of white and red *tehineh*
(value per 100 g edible portion)

Component	White *tehineh* (Sharkawy variety)	Red *tehineh* (Sharkawy variety)
Energy value *(kcal)*	708	670
Moisture *(g)*	0.6	0.8
Protein *(g)*	23.1	21.4
Ether extract *(g)*	65.1	60.3
Carbohydrates *(g)*	6.4	9.8
Crude fibre *(g)*	1.7	3.3
Total ash *(g)*	2.8	4.2
Calcium *(mg)*	134	692
Phosphorus *(mg)*	1 834	1 794
Iron *(mg)*	238	369
Thiamine *(mg)*	0.28	0.38
Riboflavin *(mg)*	0.18	0.23
Niacin *(mg)*	5.7	6.2

between grinding stones, and the resulting thick oily suspension of the ground seeds forms white tehineh.

Red tehineh is processed by sifting steeped sesame seeds (usually the Sudan variety), first in fresh water, then in 15 percent brine solution to remove the adhering dust, straw, stones, clay, etc. It is then finally washed several times with fresh water to remove traces of salt. The cleaned seeds are then roasted at a high temperature for three to four hours, till they acquire an even brown colour and a desirable flavour. They are then crushed between grinding stones to a paste consistency.

The final product is usually packed in glass or plastic jars or tins. It has a long shelf-life, since sesame seeds contain an unusual antioxidant system.

Nutritive value. Tehineh is rich in oil and proteins of high essential-amino-acids content as well as most of the B vitamins. Sixteen amino-acids were detected in the protein hydrolysate, namely alanine, arginine, citrulline, cysteine, glycine, histidine, isoleucine, leucine, lysine, methionine, phenylalanine, proline, threonine, tryptophan, tyrosine and valine. It is also a good source of calcium, phosphorus and iron (see Table 83).

Orange-blossom water
This flavouring solution is prepared by distilling flowers of rough lemon. It is widely used in the preparation of Arabic sweets and in ice cream manufacture. It is also used as a white coffee when diluted with hot water and frequently as a first aid in cases of extreme fear and fainting.

Preparation. The best stage for picking the flowers of rough lemon is when they are half open. The blossoms can be used immediately for distillation or stored for a few days. Usually the ratio of water to flower is 8:1 (w/w). The mixture is subjected to simple distillation and the aqueous distillate collected. Volatile oils that are partially soluble in the water impart a pleasant flavour to the product. This flavour improves greatly upon aging, particularly if kept for a few days in the sun. The distillate can be stored in glass bottles for several years without any preservative. The yield of distillate is usually 0.75 litres/ 1 kg flowers.

Nutritive value. This drink has no nutritive value by itself, but it is believed to slow down the rate of the heart beat, which is why it has found some medical applications in mild cases of tachycardia.

Thyme
Ground thyme *(Oryganum syriacum)* or *zaatar* flavoured with sumac *(Rumex dentatus)* is a very popular food especially among children, because of the special flavour of its main active ingredient, thymol. It is always mixed with oil (preferably olive oil) before consumption.

TABLE 84
Proximate gross composition of green thyme
(value per 100 g edible portion)

Component	Value
Energy value *(kcal)*	86
Moisture *(g)*	80
Protein *(g)*	2.8
Lipids *(g)*	0.4
Ash *(g)*	2.7
Crude fibre *(g)*	2.9
Nitrogen-free extract *(g)*	14

Preparation. Thyme species grow wild in Lebanon, the Syrian Arab Republic and Jordan. In late summer, when the flowers are mature, they are picked along with a few of the upper leaves and spread in the sun to dry well. The dried flowers are separated from the stems and ground to a coarse powder on a wiley-type mill.

Clusters of sumac, which are considered powerful acidulants, are also dried in the sun. The fruits are then ground, taking care to grind only the dried fruit pulp and not the seed. The fruits can also be hand pounded with a heavy log and then sifted. The red powder that collects is mixed with ground thyme in equal quantities, and the resulting powder is salted at the level of 2 percent. Oil and sometimes roasted sesame seeds are added to the mixture before consumption.

Nutritive value. Thyme is mainly consumed for its pleasant flavour which comes from its content of volatile oils. The major ingredient of this oil is believed to be thymol. Table 84 shows the composition of green thyme.

TABLE 85
Proximate gross composition of *mattay*
(value per 100 g edible portion)

Component	Value
Energy value *(kcal)*	491
Moisture *(g)*	3.4
Protein *(g)*	19.3
Lipids *(g)*	28.3
Ash *(g)*	0.9
Crude fibre *(g)*	4.4
Carbohydrates *(g)*	39.7

Mattay

Mattay is one of the most popular snacks available in various parts of the Gulf. Mattay has its origin in the Indian subcontinent, and is very similar to the so-called mixture in these countries. It is usually eaten as a snack between meals, but it is also served to visitors at homes. This food is composed of a mixture of different shapes of crunchy snacks, prepared mainly from chickpea flour. Peanuts and legumes, such as boiled moungpea, are usually added to the mixture.

Preparation. Chickpea flour is mixed with water, spices and salt, until a semi-liquid paste is formed. The dough is then pressed through a sieve or special container into hot vegetable oil to make thick noodles with a smooth or corrugated surface. The size and shape of the holes in the sieve are changed to produce various shapes. Roasted peanuts, chickpeas and moungpeas are added to the product, which is then packed into plastic bags.

Mattay is available on the local market, and is commercially prepared with automatic processing and packing machines.

TABLE 86
Proximate gross composition of pumpkin preserve
(value per 100 g edible portion)

Component	Value
Energy value (kcal)	398
Moisture (g)	20
Protein (g)	0.4
Lipids (g)	1.6
Ash (g)	0.7
Crude fibre (g)	1.6
Nitrogen-free extract (g)	75

Nutritive value. From the nutritional point of view, mattay is a good source of protein and calories. It is superior to other snacks commonly provided to children in schools, such as corn puffs and potato chips (see Table 85).

Pumpkin preserve

The pumpkin plant, which grows as an earthbound vine in the summer season, bears large fruits that are golden yellow to orange in colour. The fruit is very well known for its seeds, which are roasted and salted and generally consumed with alcoholic drinks.

Preparation. The pumpkins are washed and stemmed and cut in pieces using a large knife. The seeds, skins and fibrous material that may be in the centre of the fruit are removed, and the pulp is cut into small pieces, 1 cm in thickness and 3-4 cm long. The diced pulp is then soaked in 0.5 percent calcium chloride for 24 hours. Calcium ions act as a firming agent, which causes the fruit pieces to become crunchy and crisp. Excess calcium is washed away with several flushes of water, and the pulp is well drained before boiling in a hot sugar syrup. The syrup is prepared by adding a weight of sugar equal to the weight of the pumpkin pieces to twice the weight of water and boiling the mixture. The syrup is flavoured with some mastic gum and mandarine peels, which also contribute to the consistency and colour of the mix. The boiling is continued until no more vapour evolves from the syrup and the pulp becomes crisp and almost dry. The finished preserves are filled, while hot, in glass jars and stored for later use. This sweet is usually eaten as such or with cheese or cream.

Nutritive value. This food is usually consumed for its delicate and pleasing flavour. It has no significant content of nutritive elements except for carbohydrates, which make it an excellent source of food energy (see Table 86).

Bibliography

Abdel-Meguied, S.H. 1989. *Studies on hard candies*. Dept Food Science and Technology, Faculty of Agriculture, Univ. Alexandria. (M.Sc. thesis)

Abdou, I.A. & Kassim, T.A. 1978. The nutritive value, production and consumption of sesame products. *Bull. Nutr. Inst. Cairo*, 4(1): 141.

Agab, M.A. 1985. Fermented food products: "Hulu-Mur" drink made from sorghum bicolor. *Food Microbiology*, 2: 147-155.

Al-Zayani, A.R. 1988. *A taste of the Arabian Gulf*, p. 99. Bahrain, Government Press.

Aref, H. 1945. *Science of agricultural industry*. Nada press. (in Arabic)

Aref, H. 1946. *Agricultural industries*. Cairo, Nahdat Publishing Co. (in Arabic)

Assaad, S.E. 1981. *The identity of Lebanese zaatars, including a chem.-chromatographic study of their volatile oils*. Dept Biology, AUB. Beirut, Lebanon. (M.Sc. thesis)

Bressani, R. & Elias, L.G. 1968. Processed vegetable protein mixture for human consumption in developing countries. *Advances in Food Research*, 16: 1.

El-Deeb, S., Fouad, A., Krawia, S. & Khalil, S. 1956. "Halawa Taheneya". *J. of Pharmacy*, 38(12), 1956. (in Arabic)

El-Dokany, A.S. 1965. *Chemical and technological studies on sesame sweet (Halawa taheneya), chemical composition, protein value and stabilization of structure*. Dept Food Science and Technology, Faculty of Agriculture, Univ. Alexandria. (M.Sc. thesis)

El-Dokany, A.S., Mohamed M., Safwat & Aoueil, M.B. 1967. The nutritive value of sesame seeds butter (Tahena) and sesame seeds sweets *(Halawa taheneya)*. Proc. *Symp. Human Nutrition and Health in the Near East*, Beirut, Lebanon.

El-Gindy, M.M. 1964. *Food technology*. Cairo, The National Press. (in Arabic)

El-Sayed, A.F. 1965. *Chemical and technological studies on sesame seed sweets* (Halawa taheneya). Dept Food Science and Technology, Faculty of Agriculture, Univ. Alexandria. (M.Sc. thesis)

El-Shaarawy, M.I. 1967. *Studies on the preparation of local concentrates for carbonated beverages.* Dept Food Science and Technology, Faculty of Agriculture, Univ. Alexandria. (M.Sc. thesis)

El-Tayebany, Abdel-Monem, M. 1970. *Technological studies on the separation of oil from Tahena and Halawa taheneya.* Dept Food Science and Technology, Faculty of Agriculture, Univ. Alexandria. (M.Sc. thesis)

Hubert, A. 1984. *Le pain et l'olive: aspects de l'alimentation en Tunisie.* Centre régional de publication. Lyons, Editions du CNRS.

Ilany-Feigenbaum, J. 1965. Improved Halawa made with licorice extract. *Food Tech.*, 19: 216.

INS. 1975. *Table de composition des aliments tunisiens.* Institut national de la statistique. Claude Jardin, FAO Consultant, Tunis.

Kaak, Z. 1983. *La Soufra ou la cuisine tunisienne traditionnelle.* Tunis, Société tunisienne de diffusion.

Kouki, M. 1967. *La cuisine tunisienne "d'Ommok Sannafa".* Tunis, SAEP.

Leclerc, H. 1938. Sida sabdariffa *(Hibiscus sabdariffa L.). Presse med.*, 46, 1060, C.A. 33: 3891 2.

Mosleh, S. 1943. Halawa and its manufacture in Egypt. *J. Trade and Industry*, 2: 321. (in Arabic)

Musaiger, A.O. & Aldallal, Z.S. 1985. *Food consumption tables for use in Bahrain*, p. 56. Bahrain, Ministry of Health.

Pellett, P.L. & Shadarevian. 1970. *Food composition tables for use in the Middle East.* Beirut, Lebanon, American University of Beirut Press.

Sabry, Z.I. 1961. Protein food in Middle East diets in meeting protein needs of infants and preschool children. *Proc. of Intern. Conf. Washington, D.C. (1960)*

Sabry, Z.I. 1961. *Nature*, 190: 915-916.

Skipwith, A. 1986. *Askhain Saudi cooking of today*, p. 135. London, Stacey International.

Annex tables

TABLE A1
Different types of bread used to varying extents in several countries of the Near East

Name	Country	Type	Ingredients	Remarks
Armenian or sharksy	Jordan	Yeast, fermented, thick, crumby	Wheat flour	Disc-shaped, texture similar to French bread
Battawi	Egypt Sudan	Fermented spontaneously, very thin	Low-extraction-rate wheat flour, fenugreek-seed flour	Disc-shaped, long shelf-life
Corn (maize) bread	Egypt	Yeast fermented, very thin	Corn (maize) flour or mixture of wheat and corn flour	Disc-shaped, very long shelf-life
Fallahy	Egypt	Yeast fermented, very thin	Wheat flour or mixed with corn (maize) and barley flour	Disc-shaped, long shelf-life
Ftir	Sudan	Unleavened, very thin	Wheat flour	Oval to disc-shaped
Gurrasa	Sudan	Unleavened, thick (1 cm)	Wheat flour	Disc-shaped, baked on hot plate
Khobz fassan	Morocco	Yeast-fermented dough	Soft-wheat flour	Disc-shaped, 20-25 cm diameter, thick, kneaded with oil, baked
Lizzaki	Jordan Saudi Arabia	Unleavened, high moisture content	Wheat flour	Disc-shaped, grill baked
Manakeesh	Jordan	Yeast leavened, thick (1 cm), flat on layer	Wheat flour, ground thyme mix (zaatar), olive oil	Disc-shaped, breakfast meal
Markuk Maskrouh	Lebanon Syria Jordan	Yeast leavened, very thin, low moisture	Wheat flour	Grill baked, long shelf-life
Millet bread	Egypt Sudan	Fermented, very thin	Millet flour	Disc-shaped, long shelf-life
Mishtah Mankush	Lebanon Jordan	Yeast leavened, thick (2-4 cm)	Wheat flour, anise seed	Disc-shaped, sweet
Rokak	Egypt Sudan	Unleavened, thin, brittle	Wheat flour, milk	Rectangular, long shelf-life

(cont'd)

TABLE A1 (cont'd)
Different types of bread used to varying extents in several countries of the Near East

Name	Country	Type	Ingredients	Remarks
Shamsy	Egypt Sudan	Thick (3-7 cm), yeast leavened	Wheat flour, long fermentation	Disc-shaped, long shelf-life
Sfiha	Lebanon Syria Jordan	Yeast leavened, one layer, thin	Wheat flour topped with minced meat, spices	Disc-shaped, complete meal
Taboon	Jordan Syria	Yeast leavened, low moisture, one layer	Wheat flour	Baked in *taboon* on hot gravel, long shelf-life

TABLE A2
Some cereal or legume-based foods in common use in various countries of the Near East

Name	Country	Features	Ingredients	Remarks
Ajeenat baklawah	All countries	Paper-thin dough sheets, unleavened	Wheat flour dusted with wheat starch	Major ingredient in many Arabic sweets
Ajeenat knafeh	All countries	Unleavened batter formed into fine or coarse threads	Wheat flour	Baked on hot plates on rotating drums, used in preparing knafeh
Ajeenat qataief	Syria Lebanon Jordan Egypt Iraq	Chemically or yeast-leavened batter, spongy product, less than 1 cm thick	Semolina, wheat flour	Disc-shaped, filled with mixed nuts, cheese and sugar
Barazi	Syria Lebanon Jordan Iraq	Leavened or unleavened, low moisture	Wheat flour, sugar, sesame seeds, shortening	Disc-shaped, crunchy, long shelf-life
Bizir battikh	Lebanon Syria Jordan Iraq Sudan	Roasted, salted seeds	Watermelon seed	Pastinae food, seed coat usually discarded
Bizir lakteen	All countries	Roasted, salted seeds	Pumpkin seeds, salt	Pastinae food, seed coat usually discarded, rich in proteins and lipids
Jareesheh	Jordan Syria Lebanon	Raw, coarse-wheat grits	Wheat kernels	Boiled with meat or with milk and sugar
Kaak	All countries	Leavened by chickpea steep liquor or by yeast, sweetened or bland, very dry	Wheat flour, sugar (optional)	Eaten alone or with milk or tea, very long shelf-life
Korshalli	All countries	Leavened by chickpea liquor, double-baked low moisture, brittle, porous texture	Wheat flour, baking soda, sugar, shortening (optional)	Consumed with milk or tea, long shelf-life
Kusmat	Jordan Syria	Leavened by chickpea liquor, brittle, porous texture	Wheat flour, baking soda	Consumed with milk or tea, long shelf-life

(cont'd)

TABLE A2 (cont'd)
Some cereal or legume-based foods in common use in various countries of the Near East

Name	Country	Features	Ingredients	Remarks
Kallaj	Jordan Syria Lebanon	Semolina dough, very thin sheets, baked on hot plate	Semolina, water	Filled with nuts, cheese, sugar syrup
Mshat	Jordan Syria	Unleavened, runny dough, contains pieces of cauliflower, fried	Wheat flour, cauliflower, eggs	Thin discs, brown in colour, prepared by street vendors
Mutabbak	Jordan	Leavened dough, multiple layers of thin sheets	Nuts, shortening, sugar, spices and flavouring	Rectangular, studded with pine seeds, consumed as pastry
Nabet soup	Egypt	Germinated bean soup	Germinated, decorticated fava beans, onions, butter, lemon juice	
Nasha	Sudan	Fermented by lactic-acid bacteria and yeast, prepared as dehydrated powder	Millet flour, sorghum flour	Consumed as thin porridge, used as weaning food
Qdameh	All countries	Puffed chickpeas	Chickpeas, salt (optional)	Soft and yellow when dehulled (unsalted), hard and whitish when hulls retained (salted)
Sambousik	All countries	Leavened, sheeted, soft dough, stuffed with cheese or meat	Shortening, wheat flour, minced meat	Baked or fried, triangular or semi-circular in shape
Zlabieh (lokmat el kadi mushabbak)	All countries	Leavened, soft dough, deep-fat fried as balls (zlabieh), discs (mushabbak), dipped in sugar syrup	Wheat flour, potato starch	Consumed as dessert, rich in calories

TABLE A3
Some milk products produced in various countries of the Near East

Name	Source of milk	Characteristics	Countries
Akkawi	Cow	Semi-hard, white, brined	Jordan, Lebanon, Syria
Gaimer	Buffalo	Viscous liquid, 60% fat and 25% moisture, flotation cream	Iraq, Kuwait
Muddafara or *mujjaddalah*	Sheep	Hard, salted, cream-white in colour, sometimes spiced, always curly in shape	Lebanon, Sudan, Syria
Sharkasiyyah	Cow	Soft, white, acid coagulated	Jordan